D1400908

The Complete
HEALTH FOOD COOKBOOK

Exeter Books

NEW YORK

Published in USA 1985
by Exeter Books
Distributed by Bookthrift
Exeter is a trademark of Simon & Schuster
Bookthrift is a registered trademark of Simon & Schuster
New York, New York

© Marshall Cavendish Limited 1985

ISBN 0-671-07401-6

Printed and bound in Hong Kong by Dai Nippon
Printing Company

Contents

Introduction

Forget the myth that healthy eating means dull eating. You can eat deliciously well and still enjoy a balanced diet. *The Complete Health Food Cook Book* will help you keep fit and slim without starving and you will discover how much more taste good food properly cooked can have.

The important aspects of nutrition are set out in a comprehensive, practical way, with up-to-date information on vitamins, calories and carbohydrates. The dangers of sugar and saturated fats are explained and safer alternatives given. Cooking correctly is not only simpler and quicker, but we discuss the way you cook, which can affect nutritional value and flavour.

Dozens of tempting recipes throughout the book give you the chance to try things out for yourself as you go along. The ingredients may be simple and the techniques straightforward, but you are sure to be pleasantly surprised by the results. There's hours and hours of reading and eating pleasure in *The Complete Health Food Cook Book.*

Food and a New You

Vitality and radiant, sparkling, healthy good looks are among the greatest assets anyone can possess. And, amazingly, they are not elusive qualities, the gift of good fortune. Nor are they attainable only by a few exceptional people. There is no "secret formula" required and there are no shortcuts. They are the result—and the reward—of eating a diet that is nutritionally really well balanced, and, to a greater or lesser extent, everyone can enjoy them.

It is all too easy to develop lazy habits, and lazy eating habits are no exception. Attitudes towards breakfast are a good example. Most nutritionists rank breakfast as the most important meal of the day. In the morning the body is at its lowest ebb after fasting for 12 hours or even longer. A proper breakfast, rich in protein, will tone anyone up, both mentally and physically. But that extra 10 minutes in bed so often seems preferable to "wasting" time on breakfast. Consequently, a great many people have to make do with a cup of coffee before they dash out of the house.

And, all too often, this sets the pattern for the rest of the day. A sweet cake with coffee in the middle of the morning keeps the pangs of hunger quiet until lunch. Lunch is often only a sandwich eaten in haste. Then, late in the afternoon, there's a candy bar to munch and nothing else until the evening. But, after a busy day, or before dashing out to a party, it is often quicker and easier to have another nutritionally unbalanced snack meal.

So, unfortunately, even in the midst of abundance, it is possible for someone to select food that satisfies hunger or fits into a busy routine, but that still leaves him badly nourished because he has not paid attention to its nutritional content.

Everybody realises that food is vital, that human beings must eat to live and to have the energy to enjoy life. But not everybody appreciates just why food is so very important.

People really are made of the food they eat and the water they drink. Food is composed of a range of proteins, carbohydrates, fats, vitamins and minerals.

From these essential nutrients the body obtains all the raw materials it needs to grow, to maintain, to repair and replace its tissues, and for conversion into energy for work and recreation. Most foods contain only some of these nutrients and so a varied and well-balanced diet is necessary if the body is to have all the nutrients it needs, in the right proportions.

Eating a well-balanced diet can, however, mean very much more than just consuming a daily ration of nutrients. It can—and should—be thoroughly enjoyable. Food loses all its pleasant features if it is treated either as a mere routine, or as a necessary nuisance. It may be that in the future, everyone will be happy to get all the nutrients they need from pills swallowed at regular intervals.

But it is hard to imagine offering some-

Feel healthier, younger, more energetic. Enjoy the vitality and the radiant good looks which are the result and the reward of eating a well-balanced diet.

one a selection of food tablets as a gesture of affection or hospitality. For us, food has a social as well as a nutritional value. When we offer it, we are offering welcome and care.

Meals provide an opportunity to meet together as a family, or to entertain friends. Happy, relaxed company and a pleasant atmosphere can add greatly to the enjoyment of food. So can its setting. A table decorated with flowers—and lit with candles, too, for special occasions—becomes a stage on which the meal is the focus of attention.

Food generously repays the adventurousness and imagination invested in its selection, preparation and presentation. Such care may take a little more time, but that is an investment well worth making —in terms of health as well as enjoyment.

Any meal, however simple, can please not only the taste buds, but the senses of smell and sight as well. Spices and herbs give food subtle and delicious flavours

and scents, which will make even a simple meal more appetizing.

Contrasts of flavour and texture add to the interest of food because they give it liveliness. When a meal consists entirely of ingredients that are soft in taste and in texture, for example, it may be nutritionally well-balanced, but it is also uninteresting. The palate responds to small surprises—the contrast between sweet and sour, or sharp and mellow, or hot and cold. In the same way, a mixture of crisp, chewy and creamy textures makes food more real and definite.

The appearance of food is also important. A meal needs a colour scheme, but it is not necessary to give the eyes a sudden shock in order to make interesting colour combinations within a meal. The main aim—as it is with taste and texture—is contrast. A dish whose colours range from pale cream to yellow may be nutritionally faultless, but it will look dull and unappetizing. It is helpful to visualize in advance what a meal will look like when it is cooked, and the definite colours of separate ingredients become softer and blurred.

Finally, the way a meal is served can add to enjoyment. A salad arranged with care and an eye for colour is vivid and refreshing. A salad that is not arranged at all looks like a conglomeration of damp vegetables. Even the size of plate is worth attention. To someone who is dieting to lose weight, for example, a small portion on a small plate looks much more satisfying than it would if it were cowering in the middle of a large expanse of bare china. And all portions are more appetizing if they are not too large. Mounds of food look muddled and usually make people eat more than they really want or need.

These are small and simple details, but they can make all the difference between appreciating food and merely swallowing it. But, of course, absolutely essential is what is being prepared and eaten—the food itself.

Nutrient requirements vary with age, sex, body structure, amount of physical activity and other particular circum-

stances. For example, a man is often bigger than a woman, with more body tissue to repair and replace, and so he usually needs more of each nutrient in his diet. A pregnant woman, on the other hand, requires more calcium, iron, vitamins and proteins than she would normally in order to satisfy her own needs and those of the rapidly growing foetus.

Estimating an individual's precise daily nutritional requirements involves complex medical tests. But you can make an assessment of your own need for different nutrients, good enough for day-to-day use, through experiment and experience. If you use as a standard the way you feel when you are feeling very well, you will be able to adjust your diet and the amount you eat so that you are able to maintain this standard.

For most people, appetite is a fairly accurate guide to the amount of food they need. If, however, they have disturbed this natural control mechanism, which is known as the appestat, by eating too much for too long, they have to re-educate their appetite.

Nutrient requirements change with age, and, therefore, certain foods in a diet should be emphasized at different times in a person's life. Proteins, for example, are the main building units from which skin, muscle, hair, blood and the internal organs are made, and so a regular and varied supply of protein is essential during the growth period of childhood, particularly in infancy and again during the growth spurt of adolescence. A child who does not have sufficient protein will not grow and develop properly. Most people stop growing at about the age of 18, but a good supply of protein is still vital for the repair of damaged tissue and the replacement of cells worn out in use. The need for protein does not decrease with an increase in age—in fact, a shortage of protein in adult life might result in premature aging.

As a person grows older, the body requires less energy, partly as a result of the slowing down of the rate of natural chemical processes in the body—the metabolic rate as it is called—something which happens after the age of 25. It is also a result of changes in the way in which people live as they get older and the lessened opportunity or inclination to be physically very active.

Everyone needs energy, but only enough of it for the life they lead, not too much. If your energy intake is matched by energy expenditure you will maintain a steady weight. If your diet provides you with too much energy, the excess is likely to be converted into fat and stored. This will result in an increase in weight. But, on the other hand, if your diet does not provide sufficient energy, you will use up your reserves and your weight will go down.

The choice of food for a well-balanced diet or meal can best begin, from a nutritional and an economic point of view, with the main sources of protein—meat, eggs, fish, cheese and milk. Because the body cannot store protein, as it can carbohydrates and fats, each day the diet must provide enough. These same sources of protein are quite rich, too, in

Food chosen with imagination and a sense of adventure will make the well-balanced diet a pleasure to plan and to eat.

other vital nutrients. Meat and eggs contain a valuable proportion of iron, vitamins and fat. Cheese and milk provide fats, vitamins and calcium.

Vegetables or fruit not only add colour and flavour to a meal, they also provide supplementary nutrients and are a source of many vitamins. The cellulose in green vegetables, although not digested, is invaluable as roughage without which the digestive tract would not function satisfactorily.

Foods which contain a variety of nutrients should be emphasized in the diet, rather than foods containing only one nutrient, such as sugar, which is only carbohydrate, or some pure fats and oils.

Of course, carbohydrates do have a role to play in a well-balanced diet. They usually provide about half of an adult's daily energy intake. Such sources of carbohydrates as bread and cereals are often fortified with vitamins and minerals and contribute some protein. Fats, too, while adding interest to the diet, are useful sources of energy and some, such as butter and margarine, also provide fat-soluble vitamins.

A few lucky people seem to be able to eat anything and everything without putting on weight, but the majority of us have to take more care. One of the best ways of doing this is to avoid cakes, pastries, sweets and alcoholic drinks.

Individual nutritional requirements and preferences within a family or a group of people can only be covered by maximum variety in a diet, thus ensuring that each person has all the nutrients he needs while eating the food he enjoys.

It is good to drink plenty of water each day to replace that lost in urine and sweat. And tea and coffee, which are not too strong, can be drunk in any amount. The drinks to be avoided in quantity are the sugar-sweetened ones. Fresh fruit juices and cold milk are just as refreshing and much more nourishing.

Care—and above all interest—in food and its preparation are the basis of good eating habits. As the body adjusts to, and enjoys, a well-balanced diet, the longing for sweet and starchy foods vanishes and the selection of more nutritious and delicious foods becomes automatic. A well-balanced diet, based on a new approach to food, becomes, in fact, part of a way of life.

The benefits of this new approach to food and eating can be felt—and seen—amazingly quickly. It is possible to feel healthier, younger and more energetic in only a few weeks. One of the pleasures of this is hearing people say "You *do* look well". Such compliments provide a real boost to confidence and morale. But by far the greatest incentive for following a well-balanced diet is that health and vitality add immeasurably to all the other pleasures of life. There is truth in the saying "You are what you eat".

The Principles of Nutrition

All living organisms, whether animal or vegetable, need materials that build up their tissues while they are growing, and constantly make good the wear and tear of these tissues throughout their lives. In addition, they need some source of energy to carry out all the processes of life. Green plants get their building materials from the carbon dioxide in the air and from the soil while the energy comes from sunshine. Animals, including man, get both their building materials and their energy from the food they eat.

We can get a reasonably good idea of how this happens by comparing the human body to a motor car. A very special motor car, it is true, because in its first years it grows from something like a Volkswagen into something like a Rolls Royce. And, if all goes well, it keeps itself in good condition for three score years and ten, with reasonably new tyres, constantly charged battery, well-tuned engine and rust-free body.

For this to happen, you need to have two different sorts of supplies constantly available. You need all the components to keep every part of the motor car in tip-top condition, so that everything is in order and in good repair all the time. In addition, you need a source of energy both for the car to be able to run, and also to do the work of building up the car, during its growth from a Volkswagen to a Rolls, and of repairing the continuous wear and tear on its chassis and body.

You can imagine then that this very extraordinary car has to receive its supplies of material both for building and for energy from a very extraordinary kind of service station. Here there would be a special kind of pump, which would deliver a variety of supplies into a special kind of receptacle in the car. These supplies would then have to be extracted and separated into the kinds of components required by the car—rubber for the tyres, distilled water for the battery, oil for the engine, different oils for the brakes and the clutch and other moving parts, stainless steel to replace the tiny amount removed from the window frames, dozens and dozens of components, each for a different purpose.

In addition, of course, the supplies from the pump will have included petrol or gasoline, which would be used mostly for enabling the car to move, but also used to a much lesser extent for such other jobs as charging the battery, heating the car and—we must imagine—for doing the work needed for the constant repairs due to the wear of the engine and body. You can suppose that, among other things, the pump supplies crude oil, and that the car has the extraordinary ability of being able to separate this into petrol for fuel and a range of different oils for lubrication.

Of course, no car can do this by itself, but this is exactly the kind of thing that the human body can do. Each of the foods we eat almost always contains a mixture of fuel and building components. We can separate these various constituents during the process of digestion, so that when they are absorbed into the body, they circulate in the blood stream to the various tissues in the body which make use of them.

Another way in which we differ from even the most elaborate car is in our ability actively to manufacture a great number of the many components our bodies need from a much smaller number of building materials. It is as if you were able to provide the car with a mixture of a few metals like iron and chromium and aluminium, together with some silica and one or two other materials, and you then found that the car was able to make from these a wide variety of car components

The human body can be compared to a car that grows, repairs itself and moves, using food to get fuel and building components.

such as cylinder blocks, air filters, door handles and wheel hubs.

The fact is that the human body consists of several thousands of different substances. But it can make almost all of these from a large and unspecific range of other substances. There is only a small number of these that it cannot make, and it is these that make up the *essential* building materials, or nutrients—perhaps 40 or 50 of the thousands of substances which go to make our living bodies. These have to be supplied in our food, or the body will not be able to continue in health, and, indeed, may die. In other words, it is nutrients that our bodies need, but it is food that we eat.

The constituents of our food can be divided into six classes. These are carbohydrates, fat, protein, mineral elements, vitamins and water.

Water is an essential part of living tissue. Since we are losing water all the time, in the urine, from the skin, in the breath and in the stools, it must constantly be replenished. We need at least two pints every day and more—sometimes much more—if we are in a hot environment, and especially if in such an environment we are doing a great deal of physical work. While we can live for many weeks without food, we can live for only a few days without water. Normally, of course, we do not have to worry. Thirst is usually a good indication that the body needs more water. This, however, is less efficient when we suddenly find ourselves in extremely hot and exhausting conditions, where we should drink water even if we are not obviously thirsty.

As for the solid constituents of our food, some of these are used only as fuel, some are used only as nutrients, while some are used as nutrients or as fuel. The carbohydrates in our food—the starches and the sugars—are used entirely as fuel. The fat in our food is used largely as fuel, but some particular constituents of fat are nutrients. The proteins in our food are used primarily as a source of nutrients, giving the body its amino acids. But the protein not used in this way is used as fuel. Finally, the mineral elements and the vitamins are entirely used as nutrients.

We can now look more closely at the energy and the nutrients supplied by our food. The energy content of food is often referred to as its calorie content. There are two things about energy or calories that are often misunderstood. In the first place, food does not really contain calories in the same way as it might, for example, contain fat or vitamin C. You can extract the fat or the vitamin C from foods and put these into bottles, but you cannot extract calories and see them. Calories represent the energy that the food can produce when it is used as fuel in the body. In just the same way, you can, if you wish, talk of the calories in your petrol or the lead in your petrol, but while you can extract the lead, you cannot extract the calories. Until the petrol is being used to run your engine, the calories in it represent only the *potential* energy that can be released in your engine.

The second point worth making is that the word "energy" as used in nutrition does not have the same meaning as "energy" used in ordinary day-to-day conversation. When the advertisements say that Spillikins biscuits give you energy, you should not think that you eat a biscuit and this then enables you promptly to rush out to mow the lawn, or tear round the block on your bicycle. It means no more than saying that Peepbo petrol gives your car energy. Your car will not go any better by simply adding another gallon of petrol to what you already have in your tank. So to say that food gives you calories or energy is only to say that it is a source of fuel ready to *produce* energy when you "burn" it in the body.

Since all foods contain some carbohydrate or fat or protein, or a mixture of these, all foods provide energy. The chief carbohydrates are starch, ordinary table sugar and lactose. Starch is found in potatoes, bread and all cereals. Sugar is found not only in your sugar bowl, but is put by the manufacturers into sweets, cakes, biscuits, soft drinks, ice cream and a host of other foods. Lactose is a special sort of sugar found exclusively in milk.

Small amounts of other sugars in our diet come from fruit and vegetables.

The most obvious sources of fat are butter, margarine, cooking oils and fats, and the visible fat in meat. But even lean meat contains a fair amount of fat, and similar "invisible" fat is found in larger or smaller amounts in milk, fish and even bread. About half of our daily fat intake comes in these invisible forms.

We always think of protein in terms of milk, meat, fish, poultry, eggs and cheese. Certainly these foods supply a great deal of the protein we consume. But we are wrong if we think first that they contain only protein, and second that we get no protein from other foods. As we saw, meat and fish, especially fish like herrings, salmon and mackerel, contain quite significant amounts of fat as well as protein—and like most "solid" foods, quite a lot of water. Second, nearly half the protein in our diets comes from other foods. Did you know, for example, that bread contains about eight per cent of protein? Because of the amount we eat, we get on average more protein from bread than we get from eggs and fish and cheese together. This shows how important it is to consider not only how much of a nutrient there is in an ounce of food, but how many ounces we are eating.

You will remember that what we get out of proteins are their component amino acids. We then use these to build up the particular proteins we need in the body. Because of this, some of the proteins in our food are better than others, because they contain a better assortment of amino acids than do other food proteins. On the whole, most proteins from animal foods are better in this respect than are the proteins from vegetable foods. But in practice it doesn't really matter, because we eat so many different foods. As a consequence, what one protein may lack in the way of amino acids is very likely to be made up from a different assortment of amino acids from another protein. It is very rare indeed, at least in prosperous countries, for anyone to be short of protein. Each day we eat much more than the 1 or 1½ ounces that we need.

We can now look at the mineral elements and vitamins—what they do and where you find them. All of them are needed in very much smaller quantities than is protein. A day's supply of some of them is at most one-thirtieth of an ounce; of others, one-millionth of an ounce or less is all that we need for a day. Several of the vitamins and minerals are found in very many foods in more than adequate amounts, so that although they are essential, you are highly unlikely ever to be short. This applies particularly to sodium, potassium and phosphorus among the mineral elements, and pantothenic acid, pyridoxine and vitamin E among the vitamins.

Let us say a word or two about those vitamins or minerals which might be in short supply in our food. The most important mineral elements are calcium, iron and iodine. Calcium performs many functions in the body. The best known is that it is needed to build up the bones and teeth. It is found in the largest amounts in milk and cheese, but it is also found in the bones that you might eat, in sardines or whitebait, for example. Iron is chiefly used in making the colouring matter of the red blood cells. If there is not enough in the diet, the effect is to produce anaemia. The best foods for iron are meat and eggs. Iron is probably the nutrient most likely to be deficient in our lives, especially in women.

We need mention only one more mineral element, iodine. In some parts of the world, especially in mountainous areas, this was often lacking in the diet, apparently because it is washed out of the soil. The effect is to produce a swelling of the thyroid gland in the neck, called a goitre, and in children it can lead to cretinism, a disease in which there is a failure to grow physically and mentally. This sort of goitre, however, is much less common now. This is partly because some countries deliberately put iodine into their salt and also because improved transport brings iodine-rich foods, such as fish, to formerly remote areas.

The vitamins are very different one from the other, and have quite different jobs to perform. It is usual to call them by the letters of the alphabet, since when they were first discovered their chemical composition was unknown. Nutritionists today give them their chemical names, when these are known, but most people still use the letters.

They are best discussed by seeing what happens when you don't have enough of any one of them. Thus, if you lack vitamin A, you will be unable to see well in the dark. Your vision in the light will at first be unaffected, but eventually the eyes will get red and inflamed, and in due course they become so infected as to lead to permanent blindness. But this only happens in cases of severe and prolonged deficiency. Nevertheless, it does, unfortunately, happen in a number of the underdeveloped countries of the world.

Vitamin A is found in milk, butter, margarine and cheese. Especially rich sources are cod liver oil and, particularly, halibut liver oil. In addition, you are able to make vitamin A from a yellow material called carotene which is found in carrots, green leaves and some fruit.

Vitamin D is concerned with helping the body to absorb the calcium from food and to use it for making the bones and teeth. Growing infants especially need vitamin D to protect them from developing rickets. Adults require very little, if any. The amounts needed from food will depend on whether the skin has access to reasonable amounts of sunlight. This will result in the production of the vitamin in the skin. Vitamin D exists in only a few foods. Milk and butter and margarine contain small amounts, and fish-liver oils contain much larger amounts.

In the early days, a vitamin B was described which was needed to prevent beriberi, a disease found especially in people who eat a lot of polished rice and little else. We now know that the foods that protect against beriberi, especially liver and the germ of cereals, contain other vitamins, so vitamin B was divided later into vitamin B_1, vitamin B_2 and so on. The other name for vitamin B_1 is thiamine. Mild deficiency leads to weakness, constipation and, perhaps, slight paralysis, but more severe deficiency produces fully fledged beriberi. Of the other vitamins of the B group, we need mention only niacin (or nicotinic acid) and riboflavin. Insufficient niacin leads ultimately to pellagra while insufficient riboflavin leads to sore eyes and inflamed skin, especially of the face and groin.

All the B vitamins tend to be found in similar foods. Although rich sources are liver and cereal germ, you will get all you need if you include meat and milk in your diet.

Let us mention only one more vitamin —vitamin C. This is found in fruit and vegetables. Classically, scurvy was the result of diets lacking in these foods, especially during long sea voyages. It is easily lost when fruit and vegetables are sun-dried, and you yourself can destroy quite a lot by overcooking or using excessive amounts of water in cooking. Frozen fruits and vegetables, and several sorts of tinned fruits and vegetables, can still contain quite a lot of vitamin C. There is some argument as to whether a low intake, but not little enough to produce scurvy, nevertheless leads to undesirable effects. There is also some argument as to whether or not very large doses of vitamin C can produce beneficial effects such as immunity to colds.

Most of the detail about nutritional principles is of mainly theoretical interest. The best course of action is not to worry about nutrients or calories but to eat correctly. It must be remembered, however, that we do not eat nutrients or calories, we eat food. There is no need to worry about vitamins or proteins so long as you eat at least twice a day from each of the following groups:

1. Milk and cheese
2. Meat and eggs
3. Fruit and vegetables
4. Butter and margarine

You can now fill up with almost any other type of food, although you would be well advised to avoid sugar, sweet foods and drinks as far as possible.

Provided that you follow these basic principles, you should have no further need of vitamins or high-protein foods. Mankind has existed for aeons of time by eating food pure and simple without sparing a thought for its nutritional value. But, as long as your diet is sufficiently varied, and is not too full of artificial and processed food, then you should be getting all the nutrients you need without having to resort to large doses of vitamin pills.

The Nutrients in Your Food

NUTRIENTS	WHAT THEY DO	WHERE TO FIND THEM
CARBOHYDRATES Sugar	A carbohydrate, sugar is easily digested and can provide energy quickly	Sugar—fine, coarse, brown, white, icing or confectioner's Sweet foods such as cakes, puddings, chocolate, candy, jams and preserves, honey, treacle, molasses, syrup Soft drinks Fresh and dried fruits
Starch	A carbohydrate, starch is a major source of heat and energy	Cereals including wheat, maize, corn, oatmeal, rice Potatoes, arrowroot, cassava, yams Peas, beans, lentils Bread, pastry and pasta
Cellulose	A carbohydrate, cellulose forms the structural material of plant cell walls The human body is unable to digest cellulose, but it does provide valuable bulk and fibre	Present in most fruit and green, leafy vegetables Celery contains a lot of such cellulose
FATS	Provide energy and insulate the body against heat loss	Vegetable oils and shortenings, including sunflower, corn, palm, olive, coconut, groundnut or peanut, soya and kernel oils Animal fats Fish oils Butter and margarine Milk, cheese and cream Nuts
PROTEINS	Play a vital role in the growth, repair and maintenance of body tissues and provide energy	Meat, poultry, fish Milk, cheese, eggs Lentils, beans, peas
VITAMINS Vitamin A	Necessary for growth especially in children, an aid to good eyesight and healthy skin	Deep-yellow foods, such as carrots, sweet potatoes, apricots, peaches, cantaloupe. Also butter, margarine, Cheddar cheese, liver, and dark green vegetables, such as spinach and broccoli

NUTRIENTS	WHAT THEY DO	WHERE TO FIND THEM
Thiamine (B$_1$)	Assists the metabolism of carbohydrates, proteins and fats and chemical processes giving a steady release of energy	Meat, especially pork and ham, poultry Whole grain or enriched breads and cereals Eggs
Riboflavin (B$_2$)	Helps the body to get energy from food and is found in all body tissues	Milk and cheese Eggs Fish, poultry, liver and kidney Whole-grain breads, yeast and cereals
Niacin (Nicotinic Acid)	Plays an important role in growth, healthy skin and nerves. Helps the body obtain energy from food	Meat, liver, poultry, fish Milk Nut butters Bread, yeast, beans, peas
Biotin	Necessary for the health of the skin and helps liberate energy from food	Intestinal bacteria in healthy people usually manufacture enough Biotin to supply requirements, but good food sources are egg yolks, liver, kidney
Folic Acid (Folacin)	Helps in the formation of red blood cells and the reproductive system	Meat, kidney and liver Whole-grain cereals, yeast Spinach, watercress, cabbage Dried peas, beans and nuts
Pantothenic Acid	Involved in releasing energy from carbohydrates and the metabolism of fatty acids. Aids the health of the skin, growth and the production of antibodies	Widely distributed in animal tissue Whole-grain cereals, yeast Egg yolk Beans and peas
Vitamin B$_6$ (Pyridoxine)	Concerned with growth, the nervous system, fat, protein and carbohydrate metabolism and the health of the skin	Since B$_6$ is not a single substance but a collection of substances, it is available from both animal and plant sources. Liver, ham, butter beans, lima beans, yeast and corn are good sources

NUTRIENTS	WHAT THEY DO	WHERE TO FIND THEM
Vitamin B$_{12}$	Essential for the normal functioning of all cells, necessary for growth especially of nerve cells	Liver is the richest source, also meat, milk, eggs and fish. It is mostly found in foods of animal origin and therefore can be a problem for strict vegetarians
Vitamin C (Ascorbic Acid)	The main function is to assist in the formation of connective tissue, bone, skin and cartilage. It has multiple functions to do with blood vessels, red blood pigment, iron deposits, wound healing and resistance to infection	Found predominantly in green peppers, Brussels sprouts, broccoli, cabbage, cauliflower, potatoes, tomatoes, citrus fruits, blackcurrants, strawberries and cantaloupe. This is a dangerously lacking vitamin for followers of all-grain diets
Vitamin D	Vital for healthy teeth and bones, especially important in infants, adolescents, during pregnancy and during old age	Simple exposure to sunshine may fill all the required needs. Other sources of vitamin D are fish—liver oils, liver and egg yolk. Because of its scarcity in foods, margarine and butter are fortified with Vitamin D
Vitamin E	Essential for normal metabolism. There are no proven advantages to large intakes of Vitamin E, except in cases of malabsorption of fats	Wheat germ, Brussels sprouts, spinach, cauliflower, cabbage, vegetable oils, margarine, meat, eggs and nuts
Vitamin K	Essential for the normal clotting of the blood	Green leafy vegetables, cauliflower, green peas, liver, egg yolk and soya oil
MINERALS **Calcium**	Necessary for the proper development and maintenance of bones and teeth, the normal clotting of blood and the functioning of muscles. Widespread deficiency in calcium exists where iodine and fluoride supplies are low	Milk, cheese, bread, fortified flour, green vegetables, parsley Fish, such as sardines, where the bones are eaten
Phosphorus	Together with calcium it forms most of the hard structure of bones and teeth. It is involved in reproduction and the transfer of hereditary characteristics	Present in nearly all foods and calcium sources, also in meat, fish, eggs, milk and cereals

NUTRIENTS	WHAT THEY DO	WHERE TO FIND THEM
Copper	Involved in the chemistry of the blood and aids in the absorption and utilization of iron. Copper deficiencies in human beings are rare	Ordinary diets provide a sufficient supply. Good sources are liver, kidney, shellfish, nuts, raisins, cereals, peas, beans, spinach, lettuce, and cabbage
Fluoride	Incorporated in the structure of bones and teeth and necessary for the resistance of tooth decay	Fish, cheese, milk and seafoods are good sources. Water fluoridation is recommended where the fluoride level is low
Iodine	Important to the healthy functioning of the thyroid gland. Deficiency may cause goitre	Seafoods and iodized salts
Iron	Most iron in the body is present in the red colouring pigment in the blood. It is now considered the most lacking nutrient, especially among women. Deficiencies also exist where iodine and fluoride supplies are low	Red meats, especially organ meats, whole-grains, prunes, raisins, molasses, dried fruits, dark green vegetables, such as spinach, broccoli, cabbage. Also present in water and wine
Magnesium	An important constituent of all soft tissue and bone. Involved in the release of energy during metabolism	Sea salt, olives, nuts, peas, beans, cocoa, chocolate
Sodium, Potassium and Chloride	These minerals are often called electrolytes. They maintain an inner balance of body fluids. Contribute to metabolic processes	All are readily available in common foods, particularly in salt and sea salt. Frequently sodium (table salt) intake can be harmfully high
THE TRACE MINERALS Chromium, Cobalt, Manganese, Molybdenum, Silenium, Zinc and possibly others	In minute amounts these minerals are necessary for normal metabolism	Spinach, lettuce, cauliflower, cabbage, organ meats and lean meats
WATER	Water is not usually considered a nutrient, but it plays a vital role in bodily functions. It is well known that human beings can survive without food much longer than they can without water	Water or other fluids 80 to 90 per cent of fresh fruits are composed of water and 10 to 15 per cent of such foods as flour

Fats: Saturated or Unsaturated?

In recent years, there has been a considerable amount of discussion concerning the relative merits and dangers of eating saturated or unsaturated fat. Yet most people do not know what these terms really mean. Basically, if you eat soft margarine rather than butter, then you are choosing unsaturated fat in preference to saturated fat. But what is the exact difference between these two types of fat, and how does this difference affect your health?

Almost all of the fat in our diets is in the form of chemical compounds containing specific fatty acids. Fatty acids are a simple group of chemicals that may either be saturated, mono-unsaturated or poly-unsaturated. The term saturated refers to the number of hydrogen atoms in the fat. In other words, if the fatty acid has enough hydrogen atoms, it is saturated; if there is room for two more hydrogen atoms, it is mono-unsaturated; and if it can accept four or more hydrogen atoms, it is poly-unsaturated. This differing ability to deal with hydrogen atoms accounts for the markedly different properties of saturated and unsaturated fats in the body.

All natural fats contain mixtures of saturated, mono-unsaturated and poly-unsaturated fats, but these mixtures vary widely in composition. For example, butter contains on average about 66 per cent saturated fat. In contrast, soya-bean oil contains about 15 per cent saturated fat and 66 per cent unsaturated fat. Similarly, safflower oil contains about 75 per cent poly-unsaturated fat.

Generally speaking, poly-unsaturated fats are derived from liquid vegetable oils—corn, cottonseed, soya-bean and safflower oils are good examples. Margarine is another good source. (Margarine is made by bubbling hydrogen through vegetable oil. The more hydrogen the oil absorbs, the firmer it becomes. Consequently, soft margarines contain less hydrogen and more unsaturated fats than do hard margarines.) Saturated fats, on the other hand, tend to be naturally solid and of animal origin. This is frequently the visible type of fat that we eat every day—butter, lard, cream and meat fats fall into this category.

The vegetable oils contain large amounts—as much as 50 per cent—of linoleic acid, an unsaturated fat which is essential to the body for a healthy skin and proper growth. About 60 per cent of the human brain is composed of fat, of which a considerable portion is made from substances derived from linoleic acid. It is particularly important as it seems to prevent blood clotting in the final stages of the obstruction of blood vessels. Apparently it does this by preventing the blood cells from sticking together. It is absolutely vital that the diet supplies sufficient linoleic acid as our bodies cannot manufacture it themselves.

In contrast, the saturated fats may be damaging to the health. A considerable amount of evidence has accumulated which indicates that a large quantity of saturated fat in the diet can lead to the development of atherosclerosis—hardening of the arteries. This is a disease in which the arteries, especially those supplying the brain and the heart, are constricted and hardened by deposits of

Eating too much saturated fats can raise the amount of cholesterol in the bloodstream to a dangerous level.

minute particles containing a waxy substance called cholesterol. When the blood vessels become clogged with such deposits, the flow of blood decreases. This increases the chances of the formation of blood clots which block off the blood flow to the heart and brain.

Cholesterol belongs to the sterol group of fats—a different class of fats to the saturated and unsaturated types, although there is a close association between the two in their behaviour in the body. It is a normal and necessary component of the body's cells—especially of the nervous system. In fact, the body is capable of making enough cholesterol to meet its daily requirements. Thus, although some of the cholesterol eaten in the diet may be used, much of it is in excess of immediate needs. Yet many people eat a diet that is rich in egg yolks, butter and meat fats, all of which contain large amounts of cholesterol.

It has been discovered that the level of both cholesterol and fat in the blood seems to be altered by changing the composition of fat in the diet. In general, saturated fats increase the level of cholesterol in the blood while poly-unsaturated fats decrease the cholesterol level.

Clearly, the potential danger of eating

a diet high in saturated fats is that it may lead to a rise in the level of blood cholesterol. Indeed, with some people, a diet high in cholesterol and saturated fat is frequently associated with a high level of cholesterol in the blood, which, in turn, is closely correlated with mortality from heart diseases. In other words, both men and women with an elevated blood cholesterol level are more likely to have a heart attack or suffer a coronary thrombosis than those with a normal level. (This applies to women particularly after the menopause, when female hor-

mones are no longer produced in sufficient quantities to protect them). The risk increases in direct proportion to the rise in cholesterol.

There are, of course, many other potential causes of heart disease, such as stress and a lack of exercise. The relationship between heart disease and blood cholesterol levels, although close, does not conclusively establish a link between cause and effect.

Of all the factors affecting heart disease, however, it is probably easier to change dietary habits than anything else.

Since it has been proved that blood cholesterol levels can be reduced by substituting poly-unsaturated fats for saturated fats, someone wishing to lower their cholesterol level would be well advised to cut down their intake of saturated fats.

Some fat in the diet is essential. Its main function in the body is as an energy store, because it is a concentrated source of calories. This body fat also insulates us against the cold, helping to maintain a stable body temperature, and cushions our bodily organs against injury. In

Delicious as it looks, melting butter contains potentially harmful saturated fats.

addition, it is responsible for much of the pleasant flavouring in our food that makes it palatable and enjoyable, and supplies the valuable, fat-soluble vitamins A,D,E, and K.

It is not necessary to eat only the very obvious sources of fat such as butter, cream or fatty meats to obtain these benefits. In fact, this may prove to be detrimental to your health. It is wiser to obtain fats from the less obvious sources such as lean meats, cereals, nuts and vegetables. This, however, does not necessarily apply to the less obvious, invisible sources of fats such as cakes, chocolate and cheese which you may not recognize as a significant source of fats in your diet.

Therefore, saturated fats should be replaced with unsaturated fats for cooking, spreading and for adding variety and flavour to your diet. Special care should be taken to increase the amount of linoleic acid that is eaten. As all linoleic acid is derived originally from the vegetable world, this is best done by eating a wide variety of vegetables, fruits and cereals to obtain the full range of poly-unsaturated fats and their accompanying natural preservatives. (Poly-unsaturated fats are very easily destroyed when exposed to air, but are usually found naturally in combination with vitamin E which preserves them.) Fish is another excellent source of poly-unsaturated fats.

A good rule of thumb is to limit yourself to lean meat, poultry and fish and to avoid animal products that contain large amounts of saturated fats. You can gradually evolve a system of eating, mainly using unsaturated fats, that you find does not deprive you of flavour or satisfaction. Indeed, it can lead to a new appreciation of more delicate flavours if the food is not smothered by whipped cream and rich sauces.

A number of adjustments must be made when cooking meals, too. There are many excellent low-fat products available. Soft margarine, for example, can adequately be substituted for butter. While this will not help in a slimming diet, as fats of any type contain the same number of calories, it will be beneficial

Left *Fresh fish is a rare but good source of unsaturated fat in the animal world.*
Below *The seeds of the sunflower yield a valuable oil rich in unsaturated fats.*
Right *The large amounts of cholesterol in egg yolks can contribute to heart disease.*

to the health of your body. Anyway, if you do prepare meals avoiding foods high in saturated fats, you will inevitably be cutting down on your use of high calorie foods. This will give you a balanced diet that will help you to maintain a stable, suitable weight.

All you need is a change of accent in your diet. A switch to varied meals that do not include very much saturated fat will help. Butter, lard, fat meats, rich desserts, cream, ice-cream, cheese, bought cakes and pastries, chocolate and coconut should be avoided. Home-baked cakes are much better for you than store-bought ones, as you can regulate exactly what they contain—especially by using skimmed milk and soft margarine.

When eating out, stick to fish, poultry and vegetable dishes. Always avoid rich sauces and concentrate on clear soups, salads, lean cuts of meat, fish, vegetables, fruit and gelatin desserts. Pork products, beef lined with fat which cannot be trimmed away and goose should also be avoided.

Saturated fats are still on trial; they have been accused but not convicted of being the major contributory cause of heart disease. But while medical research continues into the precise relationship between fats, cholesterol and heart disease, there seems to be little point in running unnecessary risks with your health.

To minimize the risks, it is far wiser to exclude large amounts of saturated fats from your diet. It is true that many factors can contribute to the development of heart disease. But while it is not always possible to eliminate stress from your life and virtually impossible to alter a genetic tendency to heart disease, it is a very simple matter to alter your diet. Suggestions for low-fat recipes are given overleaf, using poly-unsaturated fats in preference to saturated ones. Ideally you should aim to ration yourself to one tablespoon of butter or margarine, or three tablespoons of oil a day. Similarly ½ pint of skimmed milk should suffice.

LOW FAT RECIPES

Stuffed Marrow [Summer Squash]
SERVES 2

1 medium-sized marrow [summer squash]
½ lb. lean beef, cut into cubes
2 onions, chopped
1 carrot, finely sliced
4 oz. canned tomatoes
1 clove garlic
1 teaspoon chopped parsley
    pinch of sage
2 tablespoons breadcrumbs
    salt and pepper

Preheat the oven to 350°F, Gas Mark 4, 180°C.

Melt a little butter or margarine from the daily allowance in a frying pan and add the onions, carrot, garlic, tomatoes, salt and pepper. Cook until the onions are translucent. Then add the beef, stirring constantly. Simmer for 10 minutes, adding a little water if needed. Add the parsley, sage and breadcrumbs and mix thoroughly into the meat mixture. Remove from the heat.

Clean the outside of the marrow [summer squash]. Cut in half lengthwise and scrape out the seeds. Stuff each half with the meat mixture. Place in a baking dish and cover tightly with aluminium foil. Bake in the oven for 1 hour.

Lamb Kebab
SERVES 2

½ lb. lean lamb, diced
2 slices lean bacon, cut into small pieces and rolled
2 tomatoes, sliced
2 small onions, quartered
10 button mushrooms
1 small red or green pepper
    lemon juice

Arrange the ingredients alternately on metal skewers and brush with lemon juice. Cook under the grill [broiler], turning the skewer to make sure the meat is well cooked. Serve on a bed of rice with tossed green salad.

Iced Cucumber and Chicken Soup
SERVES 2

2 chicken pieces
1 onion, diced
1 carrot, diced
1 stick of celery, chopped
    bouquet garni
    salt and white pepper
½ cucumber, cut lengthwise then thinly sliced
8-10 ice cubes

Make a stock from the chicken, vegetables and half the cucumber. When chicken is soft, strain the soup through a sieve. Cool and chill in refrigerator. Just before serving add the rest of the cucumber and the ice cubes.

Iced Cucumber and Chicken Soup is a refreshingly delicate blend of flavours that is low in fats and therefore low in calories.

Veal and Ham in White Wine
SERVES 2

    4 oz. veal, cut into thin slices,
        2-inches square
    4 oz. ham, cut into thin slices,
        2-inches square
        juice of 1 lemon
        salt and pepper
    2 oz. mushrooms
    2 tomatoes, sliced
    ¼ cup white wine
        watercress for garnish

Preheat the oven to 325°F, Gas Mark 3, 170°C.

Hammer the veal until it is very thin. Season with the lemon juice, salt and pepper. Place in a fireproof casserole dish with alternate layers of tomatoes, mushrooms and ham, finishing with a layer of tomato. Pour the wine over the dish. Cover and cook for 45 minutes. Garnish with watercress.

Pork and Sauerkraut Casserole
SERVES 2

    ½ lb. lean pork, diced
    2 onions, chopped
    1 clove garlic, crushed
    ½ tablespoon butter
    1 tablespoon flour
    11 oz. canned sauerkraut
        paprika and parsley for garnish

Cook the onion and garlic in a non-stick frying pan with a little fat from the daily allowance.

Flour the meat lightly and add to the onions. When brown, add stock or water and simmer for 1 hour.

Add the sauerkraut, stir and heat thoroughly. Garnish with a little paprika and parsley and serve immediately with a dark green vegetable.

Stuffed Peppers
SERVES 2

    2 large red or green peppers
    4 tablespoons rice
    ¼ lb. lean beef, minced [ground]
    1 onion, chopped
        lemon juice
        little marjoram or thyme
        salt and black pepper

Preheat the oven to 300°F, Gas Mark 2, 150°C.

Boil the rice, keeping it a little under-cooked. Drain. Stir in the herbs and lemon juice.

Cook the minced [ground] beef with salt and pepper and the onion, using no additional fat. After 15 minutes cooking, take off the excess fat by gently placing kitchen paper towels on the meat to absorb the fat. Throw the paper away. Add the meat and rice.

Make an opening in the peppers around the stalk. Scrape out the seeds and wash inside and out. Stuff the pepper with the meat and rice mixture. Place in a dish and cover with aluminium foil or a lid and bake for 1 hour. Serve at once on a bed of rice.

Chicken Tropicana
SERVES 2

    2 chicken pieces
        salt and pepper
    ½ teaspoon oregano leaves
    ¼ pint [⅝ cup] chicken stock
    1 small onion, sliced
    1 small courgette [zucchini], sliced
        thinly
        red and green pepper rings
        melon balls, using a ball scoop
    8 black grapes
    8 white grapes
        orange wedges

Wash and dry the chicken. Sprinkle with salt and pepper. Gently grill [broil] for 5 minutes on each side or until brown. Put in a small saucepan with the chicken stock, oregano leaves and onion. Cover and simmer until tender.

About 15 minutes before serving, add the courgettes [zucchini] and peppers. Then, with approximately 5 minutes of the cooking time left, mix in the melon, grapes and orange wedges, giving them time to warm through before serving.

Dolmades
SERVES 2

use the same stuffing as for the stuffed peppers plus:

    8 oz. canned tomatoes
    2 teaspoons basil
    1 small can vine leaves or cabbage
        leaves, blanched in boiling water

Wrap the meat and rice in vine leaves, placing 1 large teaspoon of stuffing in each leaf. Fold over the sides of the leaf and roll into a neat parcel. Place in a flat dish in rows, packing them closely together so that they cannot unroll in cooking. Sprinkle with basil and pour the tomatoes and juice over them.

Since this dish is best made with olive oil, it will make a pleasant change in the diet to use the daily allowance of fat as olive oil for this recipe.

Beef Olives
SERVES 2

    ½ lb. beef steak, thinly sliced
    2 oz. [1 cup] soft breadcrumbs
    1 large onion, diced
    2 teaspoons mixed herbs
    3 tablespoons milk
        salt and pepper

Preheat the oven to 350°F, Gas Mark 4, 180°C.

Hammer the beef steak until it is very thin. Cut into pieces about 4-inches long by 3-inches wide.

Cook the onion in a little fat from the daily allowance or in a little water. Add the mixed herbs and breadcrumbs. Moisten with the milk. Spread on the slices of beef. Roll and secure with a toothpick.

Place the 'olives' in a baking dish with a lid or cover with foil. Cook for 1¼ hours. Garnish with thin slices of gherkin to serve.

The Truth About Sugar

The sugar which you have in your sugar bowl is only one particular substance out of very many different substances that the chemist classes as "sugars." The particular sugar which you put in your tea or coffee is called sucrose by the chemist. Today all of us consume very much more of this sugar than we consume of all the other sugars in our diet put together. The commonest of these other sugars are lactose, or milk sugar, fructose, or fruit sugar, and glucose, sometimes called dextrose. Here we are talking exclusively about sucrose, because of the amounts we eat and because this is what most people mean when they talk of "sugar."

Almost all of our sugar comes from the sugar cane and the sugar beet. By the time they have been made into the refined white material we have on our tables, there is no way in which we can

The sugar in your sugar bowl may be sweet, but it is also a dangerous food which could be threatening your health.

tell whether it comes from one or the other. They are more than 99.9 per cent pure sucrose.

During the elaborate extracting and purifying processes which cane sugar undergoes, a rather crude product called raw sugar is made. It is in this form that it is largely exported from the sugar-growing countries into other countries, such as Britain, where it is refined. The raw sugar has already been very much concentrated and contains about 97 per cent of sugar, two per cent of impurities and one per cent or so of water. Its impurities are mostly dirt and unwholesome debris from the cane. The amounts of useful materials, such as vitamins and

minerals, are quite negligible. You would get more of these nutrients from a small slice of white or brown bread than you would get from half a pound of raw sugar. And you would not, surely, want to eat much of this rather dirty stuff.

Further refining of raw sugar leads to various kinds of brown sugars, although the commercially available brown sugars are often white sugar coloured with a little of the caramel produced during the refining process. All of these brown sugars have even less in the way of nutrients than does raw sugar.

White sugar has no taste other than that of sweetness. It lends itself, therefore, to the manufacture of a large range of foods and drinks, as well as to its highly acceptable use in tea and coffee. Apart from its sweetness, sugar also has a wide range of other properties that are difficult and sometimes impossible to find in other materials. It is a good

preservative, and so it is used for preserving fruits. With pectin, sugar makes jam set, as well as preserving it. It produces the glassy structure of boiled sweets or hard candies. It is because we have very pure refined sugar today that we use it in so many ways and thus consume such a lot of it.

In most industrial countries, total sugar consumption is about 100 pounds per person a year, or a little more. About 250 years ago, it was something like four or five pounds a year in Britain. By the middle of the nineteenth century, this figure rose to about 25 pounds a year in Britain. And in the United States, for which earlier figures are not available, sugar consumption was 40 pounds per person a year.

Up to about 300 years ago, sugar was a very rare and expensive commodity, imported mostly from the Far East. In the middle of the sixteenth century, it

began to be produced also in the Caribbean Islands, but even so its cost in the United Kingdom was said to be equivalent to the present-day astronomical cost of caviar. Because of sugar's attractive qualities, a great demand arose which resulted in a rapid increase in production, helped by the lucrative slave trade on the one hand, and on the other hand by the rapid and considerable technological improvements in the cultivation of the cane and the extraction and refining of the sugar.

Less than half the sugar we eat is bought as such and brought into the home. The greater part is in the cakes, biscuits, cookies, ice cream, soft drinks and other foods we buy that are already made up. There is an increasing tendency for food manufacturers to put sugar into many of their preparations, so that sugar is found not only in the more obvious foods, such as canned fruits and confectionery, but also in canned vegetables and soups, sauces and pickles, and even meat and fish products.

These wide uses of sugar help to bring our total consumption to the present high levels in the wealthy countries, where they contribute about one-sixth of the total calories of the diet. Conversely, consumption in the poorer countries has been much lower because the people cannot afford to buy so much in the way of manufactured foods and drinks. But this situation is rapidly changing. Sugar consumption in Italy before the Second World War was less than 20 pounds per person. It is now something like 75 pounds per person. There is currently a rapid increase in sugar consumption in the poorer countries of Africa, Asia and South America, as incomes rise and people can afford to buy cola drinks, biscuits, confectionery and a variety of canned foods. This tendency is increased by the increasing urbanization in these countries. Large numbers of people are moving from the villages to the large cities, where it is difficult if not impossible for them to grow their own food, so that the consumption of manufactured foods increases.

People differ greatly in their sugar

Sugar is added to baby food. Children are rewarded with sweets. Thus the hazardous taste for sugar is acquired.

consumption. Although the average consumption in the United Kingdom and the United States is about two pounds a week, there are some people who take very little indeed—perhaps not more than three or four ounces a week—while others take five pounds a week or even more. The greatest consumption seems to be by teenage boys. Consumption falls off with increasing age, and at any given age girls and women, on average, take less sugar than boys and men.

It seems pretty certain that people develop a taste for sugar, not to say a craving. As they get used to having sugar in their dishes and to eating sugary foods, they seem to demand more and more, until some of them consume quite large amounts. The converse is certainly true.

Those people who for any reason reduce their sugar consumption soon find that they no longer like sweet foods, cannot take sugar in their tea or coffee, and find ice cream and many sorts of confectionery distinctly unpleasant. The cultivation of the taste for sugar begins in infancy, when mothers add sugar to many of the milk formulas for bottle-fed babies, give them sugar water or sweetened fruit juice when they are thirsty, and sprinkle sugar on their cereal or even on their egg yolk or meat when they begin mixed feeding.

At this point it is reasonable to ask whether our present high consumption of sugar has any advantage or disadvantage in terms of health. Certainly, most people like sweet foods, or at least a touch of sweetness in their food. We find that most tinned vegetables have sugar added to them, and most of the tins and jars on the shelves of the supermarket labelled "new" are likely to be basically the same mixture as before, but with added sugar. This is true, for example, of many brands of tomato juice, peanut butter, pickles and sauces.

In so far as people eat foods that they like rather than foods that they don't like, you can say that the added sugar has an indirect nutritional value. If the sugar makes you eat the tinned peas that you otherwise would not eat, you get the protein and vitamins and other nutrients of the peas that you would obviously not get if you did not eat them. Here sugar obviously imparts a nutritional advantage. But you can at once see that the same high palatability that the sugar confers could also persuade you to take food and drinks that do not necessarily supply the sorts of nutrients that tinned peas do. You could be taking a cola drink or an "orange" drink that contains little or no nutritional value, apart from that of the sugar itself. This is true of the majority of foods, especially those that have a high content of sugar. Most confectionery, cakes, biscuits and ice cream do provide some protein and minerals, but very little indeed in proportion to the calories they give.

It is important to remember that sugar gives you calories and *nothing but* calories. It is absolutely free of protein, vitamins and mineral elements. For most of us, extra calories are just what we do not need. With half the adult population overweight, and an increasing number of overweight infants and children causing much concern to doctors, we have to try to limit our calories in food, but without, of course, limiting the nutrients. This, then, is the first and most obvious disadvantage of sugar—it helps to make us overweight. We like our sweets and soft drinks and cakes so much that we take them for pleasure, and not because we need more calories.

It is possible, of course, if we have an excellent appetite-controlling mechanism, that sugar does not make us overeat. It could be that we then eat less of our other foods to just the extent that we eat sugar. But we now have to face the danger of a reduction in the quality of our diet. Any food other than sugar gives us not only calories but also nutrients. So if we, for example, take 25 per cent of our calories as sugar (and many people take more than this) and push out of our diet an equivalent of other foods, our intake of protein, vitamins and minerals will be reduced by the amounts that these other foods contain.

Apart from producing overweight, or reducing the nutritional value of our diets, there are several other disadvantages in eating the amounts of sugar that we do. Sugary foods that tend to stick to the teeth are the most potent cause of dental decay. In Britain, for example, more than four million teeth are extracted each year. The bacteria that produce the acid that causes tooth decay flourish much better in sugar than in any other food material.

These situations are all quite easy to understand and to demonstrate. Fat people who give up the sugar they eat will lose weight. Diets that are only marginally nutritious when they contain sugar become better balanced when the sugar is removed. Children who do not eat sweets and sticky buns and biscuits have much less dental decay. There are, however, other and much more complex diseases where the evidence is not so clear-cut, although research is increasingly incriminating sugar as a cause.

The most important of these diseases is what is commonly called coronary thrombosis. This is now the chief cause of death in most industrial countries. In Britain and the United States, one man out of three over the age of 40 is likely to die from a heart attack involving the coronary arteries. It is far commoner in well-off countries than in the poor countries, and it is now very much more prevalent than it used to be. It is generally agreed that coronary thrombosis has several causes, among which are cigarette smoking and lack of exercise, both characteristics of the affluent society.

It is very likely, too, that dietary indiscretion is a cause, and for many years it has been suggested that this is an excessive consumption of animal fats and cholesterol. Animal fats are those found in meat, and in milk, butter and cream. Cholesterol is found mostly in eggs. Whether or not these foods are involved is still debated today. In the meantime, there has been a great deal of new research that suggests that sugar is a possible cause of this disease. The arguments are many. The disease is more common in countries where consumption of sugar is high. The biggest dietary change over the period where the disease has become so common is the enormous increase in sugar consumption. Giving sugar to laboratory animals and to human volunteers produces abnormal-

Sugar gives you calories and nothing but calories. It is totally lacking in proteins, vitamins and minerals.

ities in the blood similar to those seen in people with heart disease.

A disease that has also increased, although not so alarmingly, is diabetes. It is especially interesting because it is linked with heart disease. People with one condition are more likely to have the other condition as well. Experiments have shown that people and laboratory animals given a lot of sugar to eat, produce the same sort of difficulty of dealing with their own blood sugar (glucose) that is seen in diabetes. It has also very recently been shown that if you breed from those rats that develop the greatest impairment in glucose metabolism when given sugar, in three generations you obtain a strain of rats that are quite normal if sugar is left out of their diet, but develop full diabetes when sugar is put into their diet.

There are several other diseases in which sugar may play a part. These include chronic indigestion (like that met with in gastric and duodenal ulcers) and a common skin condition called seborrhoeic dermatitis. But people begin to get rather sceptical when you mention the possibilities that one simple substance, sugar, can really be involved in causing so many conditions.

One reason, of course, is that most people like sweet foods and drinks, and so resist the idea that something as nice as this can also be harmful. A second reason for scepticism is that most of us have been brought up to believe that sugar is just another carbohydrate. The only difference, we thought, between sugar and starch—the other major carbohydrate in our diet—was that sugar was more quickly absorbed. The fact is, however, that ordinary sugar (that is, sucrose) is digested to yield equal amounts of glucose and fructose, whereas starch is digested totally to glucose. There is now no doubt that fructose produces a large number of undesirable changes in the body, quite different from those produced by glucose.

The most important reason for believing that sugar may be involved in a number of diseases is the fact that it produces quite large increases in the amounts of several potent hormones circulating in the blood stream. It is interesting to compare this *real* effect of sugar with the concern that many people have for the supposed effects that may be caused by the use of hormones in animals for meat production. The amount of the hormones that get into the edible parts of the animals is almost undetectably small, and the amount that would get absorbed into the consumers' blood stream would be very little indeed, if any at all.

It is said that sugar is good because it is such a quick source of energy. Energy here means nothing more than calories. And all food, without exception, supplies calories. Nor is there any advantage in having this energy quickly. First, every person always has more than an adequate store of energy in the liver, muscles and fat of his body, unless he has been starving for weeks. Second, the fact that the products of sugar digestion are more rapidly absorbed than the products of starch digestion is not necessarily a good thing. The resulting rapid fluctuations in the levels of blood sugar may, for example, be responsible for the condition known as hypoglycaemia, where people feel faint and weak some time after a meal, and may actually faint.

If, very sensibly, you are going to give up sugar as much as possible, what about alternatives? At present the only alternative general sweetener is saccharine. So if you must have sweet tea or coffee or fruit salad, you will have to use this. There is, of course, the possibility of using honey instead of sugar for at least some foods. It has no nutritional advantage over sugar, in spite of all the magic things that are claimed for it. On the other hand, for most people, honey is unlikely to do as much harm as sugar does, because they are very unlikely to be able to eat anything like the two or three pounds or more of sugar a week that so many people consume.

One thing is worth repeating. This is that, apart from its taste, sugar does nothing for you that is not done better and with less danger by any other food. The physiological requirement for sugar is nil. The body can do very well without any sugar at all added to any foods or drinks.

Eating for Health

If you feel sluggish, depressed or have frequent headaches and colds it all could be due to the way you eat. Instead of taking unnecessary medication or spending a lot of money trying to hide blemished skin or broken nails with cosmetics, examine and change your eating habits. It could make all the difference.

The need to eat a sensible, well-balanced and nutritionally-sound diet can never be over-emphasized. Food is the fuel that makes the body run well. When you neglect your diet, you are harming your system in some way. Each vitamin, each mineral, every gram of protein consumed has some effect on the body and the failure to eat enough of any one of the essential nutrients can have an adverse effect on your general health and

well-being. It is vital, therefore, to know just what constitutes good eating habits. Learning what to eat and how to eat it is very simple, and it is certainly worth the effort.

Eating a wide variety of foods is best. No one food is responsible for the maintenance of the body and eating too much of one thing can be harmful as you tend to do so to the exclusion of other necessary nutrients. You must learn to enjoy eating what is good for you. Sweet foods may be very soothing and gratifying, but they do little to help you look and feel better. And a slice of cheese may prove just as comforting to eat, while at the same time adding to the daily protein intake. Good eating is not dull eating. Think about what you eat.

Time and money are constantly wasted on food that is not beneficial to health and vitality. Change bad food habits now and you will feel the benefits for the rest of your life.

Each type of food is responsible for the care of a different part of the body, and the total absence of any important nutrient can cause a disturbance in the body processes. Sluggishness and lack of energy can often be traced to some kind of diet deficiency. Irregular, badly planned meals also lead to a disruption of the digestive system, and this can cause constipation. Constipation clogs up the bloodstream with waste materials and can result in poor circulation and blemished skin.

To eat properly, it is advisable to have

three balanced meals each day—but you may also have snacks in between meals. The best snacks are fresh fruit or a glass of fruit juice. These raise the blood-sugar level without adding the high concentration of sugar—found in sweets, cakes and buns—which can easily overload the bloodstream.

To illustrate the tremendous difference in appearance and health that diet can make, look at the eating habits of two young girls. Girl A eats well. Her diet consists of fresh fruit, vegetables, lean meat, fish, dairy foods and salads. She always eats a reasonably good breakfast and takes regular meals at regular times. When she goes out to dinner and eats more than usual, she restricts her carbohydrate intake the next day and eats more fruit. She drinks water, milk, a little tea and coffee and a little alcohol. This girl has health, good looks and vitality. Common ailments do not often trouble her and she shakes off colds easily.

Girl B eats badly. Her diet consists of snack foods, fried meals, sandwiches, cakes, confectionery, plus the occasional tray meal. She eats few vegetables and little fruit. She drinks sugar-loaded soft drinks and alcohol. She takes very little exercise. Her skin is spotty due to lack of vitamins B and C and her figure is spreading. This girl not only looks unattractive, but her health is slowly deteriorating as well. Her teeth have more 'filling' than enamel. She feels sluggish and depressed, has little energy for social events and is inefficient and tired at work. This is all due to the lack of nutrients in her diet.

These two girls demonstrate the importance of a proper diet. They eat approximately the same amount of food, but one eats sensibly whereas the other does not—and the results are visible.

Everyone needs to eat regularly, meat, fish, or poultry in addition to cheese, salad, green vegetables, fresh fruit and vitamin-enriched bread. The correct amount of calories must be consumed, and excesses of fat and carbohydrate should be avoided. The most important thing is to be sure that you have adequate amounts of protein, vitamins and minerals in your diet.

Protein is responsible for the building and repair of the body and is found in fish, cheese, meat and poultry. Organize the main meal of the day around one of these. Nuts and yogurt are also good sources, and can be used throughout the day to supplement your intake. A man in a moderately active job needs at least one full meal based on protein per day, a woman needs only slightly less. Children need the greatest amount, as their bodies are still growing. Babies get all the proteins they need from milk. Additional protein may be needed by adults after an

Buy fruits and vegetables fresh each day. They lose essential nutrients like vitamins C and B when they are stored.

24

illness or for the healing of serious wounds.

Vitamins are also an essential part of the well-balanced diet. There is a lot of research now being done on the nature of vitamins, the varied effects they have on the body and the validity or otherwise of the benefits claimed to be derived from them—in particular vitamins E and B. Nonetheless, a lot is already known about the body's vitamin requirements.

Vitamin C strengthens the body's resistance to many minor illnesses and is good for the skin and gums. It is also necessary for building up the blood and for forming the substance which holds body cells together. The vitamin C level is kept up by eating oranges, grapefruit and green vegetables. The body cannot store this vitamin so a sufficient intake of it is needed each day.

Skin also needs vitamin B_2, which is found in fresh vegetables, milk and wholewheat bread. Teeth and bones need calcium and vitamin D, obtained from milk, fish oils and yeast.

Eyes need vitamin A to help the retina function properly and prevent night blindness. Vitamin A also maintains the delicate linings (called mucous membranes) of the tracts of the digestive, respiratory, urinary and reproductive systems. The function of these linings is to protect the tissues beneath them from damage or infection. Cabbage, carrots, butter, eggs and fish-liver oils are the best sources of vitamin A.

The vitamins of the B complex, found in lean meat, liver, fish, wheat-germ and milk, build up the blood and thus prevent anaemia. Anaemia can result in fatigue, breathlessness, and general loss of vitality.

Mineral substances in food are vital, for in many cases they actually trigger off the action of the vitamins. Their importance is only just being realized, particularly that of the 'trace' minerals which, although present in foods only in minute quantities, are essential to health. Iodine is a trace mineral found in sea food. It affects the thyroid gland, and lack of it can cause a disease called goitre, resulting in a swelling of the neck, and in more severe cases, accompanying disfigurement of the eyes and face.

Calcium is the mineral which is essential for all bone development and maintenance, and is found in milk, cheese, sardines and molasses. Iron is contained in egg yolk, liver, peanuts and some green vegetables. It is very important for women during the child-bearing years because it builds new blood cells. Many women fail to eat enough iron-rich foods to replace the blood lost through menstruation. A deficiency of iron in the diet can cause dark shadows under the eyes, a pallid complexion and a lack of vitality and vigour.

To aid in the digestion and excretion of this well-balanced diet, roughage is also needed. Roughage is contained in some green vegetables and cereals.

Organize your main meal around protein, which is needed by the body for growth and repair. Meat is an excellent source.

Salads are also an excellent source.

Unfortunately, it does not follow that if you eat a lot of a particular food it will do you even more good. Certain foods should be avoided in excess. Fried foods are not beneficial to health or weight and are bad for the skin. Highly-spiced or curried foods can, over a long period of time, lead to ulcers. And it may be wise to avoid eating too much cholesterol (animal fat)—found in high concentration in egg yolk—because it is believed to be a contributing factor in heart disease and hardening of the arteries in people over 30.

Excess acid in the system causes kidney trouble, headaches, numbness of the feet or hands, burning urine and pain in the joints. Sugar, used in combination with fruit, produces acidic results. Cooking fats increase the acidity of food. Egg-yolk and oysters are particularly high in acid-forming content, and cakes and confectionery are also quite acidic.

An overall good diet would be low in sugar and starch and high in protein and vitamin-rich foods. The only organ in the body that requires glucose (sugar) is the brain, and enough glucose can be produced by the body from other foods to fill that requirement. An excess of starch or carbohydrate in the diet leads to weight gain, as the body will convert it into fat and store it. In addition to being unattractive, weight gain is unhealthy. It can lead to heart disease, hernias and varicose veins.

While watching what you eat, you must also make sure that you eat enough. Energy is measured in units called calories, and each person requires a certain amount of calories every day. The number of calories you need is dependent upon your size, job and metabolic rate. The metabolic rate indicates how quickly the body utilizes the food consumed. Everyone has a slightly different rate of utilization. This accounts for the fact that some people can eat large amounts and never gain weight. Others eat small amounts and continue to gain weight because their bodies do not use the food quickly and hence the food is stored in the body in the form of fat. So try to judge your metabolic rate and eat accordingly.

Maintaining good eating habits and proper exercise is the only way to be sure of remaining healthy and fit. If you neglect your diet, your body will be damaged and you will notice the difference in your appearance and health. Always watch the number of calories in food, have adequate amounts of protein, vitamins and minerals and do not consume too much fat or too many carbohydrates. Make these simple rules of good eating part of your daily routine and you will be pleasantly surprised at the difference they will make.

The Versatile Egg

What is a square meal in an oval shape? The answer is an egg. No other food contains so many nutrients essential for life and radiant good looks in such a beautifully designed package. Eggs really are the best kind of food—packed full of goodness, quick and easy to turn into a satisfying meal and invaluable aids in all forms of cookery.

In some countries there are more hens than people, which means that eggs are plentiful, generally cheap and excellent value for money. And slimmers can eat eggs without feeling guilty—they contain absolutely no sugar and only a trace of fattening carbohydrate.

Eggs are good for you
It's astounding how much goodness is found in just one egg. An egg is basically a chicken in embryo form, so naturally it contains everything necessary for life, growth and healthy upkeep of blood, bones and tissues.

Just one medium-sized egg will provide over seven per cent of your daily protein requirement but only about three per cent of your total calorie intake. Add to this the fact that the same egg will give you over three per cent of your daily calcium, about 11 per cent of your iron, 10 per cent of your vital Vitamin A and Carotene, four per cent of Thiamine (Vitamin B1) and nearly 10 per cent of Riboflavin (Vitamin B2). . . . And then there are the many other valuable health-giving elements such as sulphur, magnesium and chlorine . . . . Egg-protein is of a particularly high quality—good for building strong bones and teeth, keeping skin clear, nerves in good working order and general health superb. Eggs don't, however, contain any Vitamin C—so plan your diet with this in mind. (Adding tomatoes—which are rich in Vitamin C—to eggs will give you a low calorie, perfectly balanced meal).

Eggs are easily digested which is why they are specially recommended for young children, invalids and old people who have difficulty chewing and digesting solid food. They can be beaten up

raw in milk, fruit juice or even sherry for an easily assimilated and pleasant tasting meal—an excellent idea for a rushed snack, too.

Eggs for use
Cooking with eggs is a sure way to produce interesting and nutritious meals. Eggs, used in cake-making ensure a light, fluffy texture and creamier taste; they keep oil in emulsion for a really smooth mayonnaise; they bind food together as in potato croquettes; they form a protective film to prevent food absorbing fat during deep frying and they thicken sauces and custards.

If you keep a supply of eggs handy in the kitchen you'll never be at a loss for a meal.

Simple egg cookery
Eggs are still mainly thought of as food—primarily breakfast or snack food, when a boiled or fried egg will 'fill a gap' without much care or imagination being required. We tend to think of cooking eggs as being the easiest job in the kitchen. A common phrase of scorn for a hopeless cook is 'she can't even boil an egg'. Yet the basic methods of cooking eggs are more difficult to master than you think. Everyone knows the irritation of

Eggs are packed full of health-giving protein, vitamins and minerals — and contain only a little fattening carbohydrate.

being faced with an over-or under-boiled egg, scrambled eggs with whey oozing out or rubbery fried eggs. Learning how to avoid these disasters is simple:

First the egg should be fresh. You can test this by breaking the egg into a saucer. If the yolk and surrounding white is raised into a dome-shape then it is very fresh. If it is raised at all it is reasonably fresh, and if it's as flat as a pancake it's dubious. One or two tiny specks of blood on raw egg are nothing to worry about, and a coil of white fibrous material is simply nature's device for holding the egg to the shell.

But any other discolouration and certainly any smell means that the egg is 'off' and should be thrown away. It's a good idea when making dishes which require more than one egg, to break each one separately into a saucer in case one is bad and contaminates the others.

Boiling an egg
Eggs should be lowered into enough water to cover them completely. The water can be cold or boiling, but always start timing from the instant the water begins to boil. Ideally eggs should be boiled gently to prevent them banging together and cracking in the pan, and to avoid over-cooking which makes them rubbery and sometimes forms a dark greenish ring where the egg yolk meets

with the egg white.

Small eggs should be boiled for 3½ minutes, medium-sized eggs for 4 minutes and large eggs for 4½ minutes to produce firm whites and semi-liquid yolks. Remember that even if you remove the pan from the heat, eggs will go on coagulating in the hot water, so take them out immediately.

Small eggs take 2½ minutes to soft-boil, medium-sized eggs take 2¾ minutes and large ones take 3 minutes. This will give you a runny yolk and semi-liquid white.

It's a good idea to be precise about egg-timing. Hard-boiled eggs cook for so long you might either forget about them until they're stuck to the bottom of the pan or else take them out too soon. Use an egg-timer or remember to keep a check on your watch—the second hand will be invaluable—to obtain the best results. A small egg takes 8 minutes to

hard-boil perfectly, a medium-sized one 9 minutes, and a large one a full 10 minutes.

Keep boiled eggs warm the old-fashioned way—colourful knitted egg cosies are both attractive and effective.

Frying eggs
The perfect fried egg should have firm white and a creamy yolk which can have a white film over it (according to taste). Disasters include fringes of burnt white, tough yolks over-running their banks and a sort of greasy two-tone pancake. Remember one of the reasons eggs are fried is because it's a quick way of making them palatable—so don't overcook them.

Eggs can be fried in a variety of fats. Which one you use depends on whether you want your eggs to taste of the fat or just to taste of eggs. Bacon fat is particularly tasty but don't use olive oil unless you know you like its taste. Frying in butter always gives eggs a round, satisfying flavour and the butter can be spooned over toast to give the meal an added boost. You can also add wine to the butter or vinegar flavoured with

herbs or sherry to lift the dish out of the ordinary. And as with any fried food your briskly fried egg must be 'blotted' on a bed of kitchen paper before serving to remove the last vestige of sickly grease.

Scrambled eggs
Eggs are the only foods you can scramble, so it's worthwhile establishing a workable and fool-proof method of reaching the best results every time. Scrambled eggs are good by themselves or as traditionally served—on buttered toast or fried bread, and they are delicious accompaniments to a variety of hot, buttered vegetables to make a hearty and economical meal.

Most people have their own methods of scrambling eggs, but a simple way of getting good results is: break a practical number of eggs into a bowl. Two to eight, depending on the number of ravenous guests you have waiting is the usual sort of quantity. Break the yolks up into the whites with a fork—but don't whisk, or you'll end up with an omelette. Add a pinch of salt and pepper. For a smoother texture, add a knob of butter or a tablespoon of cream but they're not absolutely essential. Put the pan on moderate heat then stir gently, taking care to include all the eggs as you stir. When there is still a little semi-liquid egg in the pan remove it from the heat and let it solidify with its own heat. The eggs should have a light texture with even flakes of egg and no extra liquid.

Try splitting a hot baked potato and piling it high with scrambled eggs and wedges of raw tomato. Or adding slivers of tomato, a pinch of mixed herbs and half a clove of chopped garlic to the eggs as you cook them. Cubes of cooked ham, or rolls of crispy bacon add 'body' to the meal. Or flakes of fish and raw peppers, some chopped chives and onions take only minutes to change an everyday meal into something special. And grated cheese always provides an interesting flavour.

Poaching eggs
Poached eggs are deceptively simple. Even if you don't own a poaching device you might think that poached eggs are simply a matter of cracking an egg into boiling water and keeping your fingers crossed. Only too often the eggs come out of the pan in watery shreds and not very presentable.

The best way is to heat about three inches of water in a medium sized pan and swirl the water around. Drop an egg into the vortex so that the egg keeps a good, round shape—but don't expect to get perfect results the first time. Or the tried-and-tested way is to slide the egg gently into bubbling water and roll it with a spoon to keep it together. A few drops of vinegar or a pinch of salt will help to keep the egg together in the pan but of course they tend to add a vinegary or salty flavour which you might not want. Poaching eggs in milk is a nutritious way to make a meal—especially valuable for

invalids. Serve the eggs as usual with toast or croutons.

Making omelettes
A well-made omelette makes a quick and delicious meal. Although they are basically very simple, omelettes are surrounded by an undeserved mystique. The secret is not to overcook them and to do everything quickly with a light, firm hand.

Break two or three eggs into a bowl and whisk them thoroughly. Water or butter isn't necessary though you could add small quantities of both if you wish. Add a pinch of salt and pepper to taste.

Melt a large knob of butter in a pan—preferably a special omelette pan kept just for the making of omelettes and nothing else. Pour the mixture into the pan and keep the heat moderate and constant. Using a wooden utensil stir the centre of the omelette a little—just enough to stop it sticking. Tilt the pan from side to side and lift up the sides of the omelette so that the uncooked mixture can get to the centre. When all the egg is cooked loosen the omelette with a quick flick of your wrist and fold it over to form a 'turnover' shape. Serve it on a warm plate garnished with watercress and quarters of raw tomato.

There is no end to the variation on this theme and the various fillings. Try making a cheese omelette by piling the cooking mixture up with grated cheese and waiting until it's just melted before folding it over, and pouring either extra melted cheese or properly thickened cheese sauce over the top. Slices of cooked potato and shred of ham, or even sliced, continental sausage with a dash of sweet and sour sauce will make a pleasant change.

Omelettes always go well with crisp, green salads so try to ring the changes with the ingredients of the salad, too. Contrast the flavour and texture of the eggs with walnuts or crispy red cabbage, sliced green peppers and slivers of succulent endives. Other interesting accompaniments to a plain omelette are courgettes or zucchini cooked with garlic, braised onions and creamed potatoes, or tomatoes stuffed with sweet corn kernels.

Coddling eggs
Coddled eggs are basically very lightly boiled—suitable for someone who has difficulty chewing and digesting food, and they can tempt the appetite when all else fails because they seem so light and packed full of goodness.

Just put eggs into boiling water, cover and take the pan off the heat and leave for roughly 7 or 8 minutes. The eggs should be soft but edible and easily eaten with a spoon.

There are many more ways of cooking eggs, but whichever technique you prefer, you can be sure that you are getting the best value for money in terms of flavour and nutrition.

Baked Alaska

An impressive dessert, Baked Alaska is sponge cake topped with ice cream and covered with meringue. It is not difficult to prepare but it does need very speedy, last-minute preparation before serving.

6 SERVINGS

1 tablespoon butter
3 oz. [¾ cup] plus 1 tablespoon flour
6 oz. [¾ cup fine] plus 1 tablespoon castor sugar
4 egg yolks, at room temperature
4 egg whites, at room temperature
1 teaspoon vanilla essence
1 teaspoon baking powder
¼ teaspoon salt
8 oz. [¾ cup] apricot jam
2 pints vanilla ice-cream, softened

MERINGUE
6 egg whites
⅛ teaspoon salt
6 oz. [¾ cup fine] castor sugar

Preheat the oven to moderate 350°F (Gas Mark 4, 180°C). Grease two 8-inch

Tasty ways with Eggs

sandwich tins with butter.

Mix the 1 tablespoon of flour with the 1 tablespoon of castor sugar in a cup and dust the greased sandwich tins with the mixture. Shake out any excess flour and sugar.

Put the egg yolks in a medium-sized mixing bowl. Add the vanilla essence and beat with a wire whisk or rotary beater until the mixture is pale and thick. Add the sugar, reserving 4 tablespoons, and beat to mix.

In another mixing bowl beat the egg whites with a wire whisk or rotary beater until they form soft peaks. Add the reserved 4 tablespoons of sugar a spoonful at a time and continue beating until the whites are stiff.

Fold the beaten egg whites into the egg yolk mixture, with a metal spoon, until they are well mixed.

Sift the remaining flour with the baking powder and salt into the egg mixture and fold in with the spoon.

Pour the mixture evenly into the two cake tins and bake in the centre of the oven for 20 to 25 minutes or until the cakes are done. Test the cakes by inserting a skewer into the cakes, if it comes out clean the cake is cooked. Turn the cakes out carefully on to a rack to cool.

When the cakes have cooled spread one cake with the apricot jam. Put the second cake on top of it. Trim off the corners of the cake with a knife to make an oval shape.

Put the ice-cream on a sheet of aluminium foil and mould it gently to the size of the cake. Cover it with foil and place it in the freezing compartment of the

refrigerator to become hard.

Preheat the oven to a very hot 450°F (Gas Mark 8, 230°C).

In a medium-sized bowl, using a balloon whisk or rotary beater, whip the egg whites and salt until they are stiff. Beating continuously, add the sugar a little at a time. Continue beating until the whites are stiff and glossy. Do not overbeat or the whites will begin to collapse.

Put the cake on a flat baking sheet. Remove the ice-cream from the refrigerator, take off the foil and place the ice-cream on top of the cake. Using a spatula, cover the outside of the cake and the ice-cream with the meringue mixture, making sure that there is no cake or ice-cream showing. This must be done very quickly and the meringue must cover the ice-cream and cake completely or the ice-cream will melt. As an added decoration toasted almonds may be sprinkled on to the meringue.

Put the baking sheet in the centre of the oven and leave it for 3 to 4 minutes until the meringue turns a pale golden colour. Serve at once.

Castilian Omelette

An interesting variation on the basic omelette, Castilian omelette is a tempting filling mixture of potatoes, onions and eggs. Unlike the traditional French omelette, this is not folded over but is served flat and cut into wedge-shaped pieces. It may be served with a courgette [zucchini] salad.

4 SERVINGS

5 tablespoons olive oil
3 medium-sized potatoes, peeled thinly sliced and dried on kitchen paper towels
1 large onion, finely chopped
½ garlic clove, crushed
¼ teaspoon salt
4 eggs

In a large frying-pan, heat 4 tablespoons of the oil over moderately low heat. When the oil is hot, put in the potatoes, onion, garlic and salt. Fry them slowly for 20 minutes, or until the potato slices are cooked and lightly browned on both sides. Remove the pan from the heat. With a slotted spoon, remove the pota-

toes and onions from the pan. Set aside on a warmed plate.

Pour off the oil from the pan. Wash and dry the pan.

In a medium-sized mixing bowl, lightly beat the eggs with a fork. Add the potato and onion mixture to the eggs and stir gently so that the ingredients are well mixed, taking care not to break the potato slices.

Preheat the grill [broiler] to moderate.

Pour the remaining oil into the cleaned frying-pan and place it over moderate heat. When the oil is hot, pour in the egg-and-potato mixture. Tip and rotate the pan so that the mixture covers the bottom of the pan completely.

Cook the omelette for about 5 minutes, or until the underside is golden brown. Shake the pan occasionally so that the omelette does not stick.

Remove the pan from the heat and place it under the grill [broiler]. Cook for 2 to 3 minutes, or until the top is firm and evenly browned.

Slide the omelette on to a warmed serving dish and serve hot.

Apricot Condé

A classic French dessert, Apricot Condé is easy to make and is an elegant dessert to serve, hot or cold, at a dinner party.

6 SERVINGS

1 teaspoon salad oil
4 oz. [¾ cup] rice
1½ pints [3¾ cups] milk
4 oz. castor [½ cup fine] sugar
1½ tablespoons butter
a pinch of salt
1 teaspoon vanilla essence or ½ vanilla pod
6 egg yolks
6 oz. [¾ cup] granulated sugar
15 fl. oz. [2 cups] water
1 lb. fresh apricots, peeled halved and stoned
2 tablespoons kirsch

Preheat oven to moderate 325°F (Gas Mark 3, 170°C). Lightly brush the inside of an 8-inch soufflé dish or mould with salad oil.

In a saucepan, wash the rice thoroughly under running water until the water runs clear. Drain the rice and put it in a flameproof dish with the milk, castor sugar, butter, salt and the vanilla essence, or pod, and bring to the boil over high heat. Stir until the sugar is dissolved and the ingredients are well mixed.

Cover and place the dish in the centre of the oven for 30 minutes, or until the rice is cooked.

Take out the vanilla pod. Lightly beat the egg yolks and mix into the rice. Place the rice in the soufflé dish or mould. Cool, cover and place in the refrigerator until cold.

To make the sauce, put the water and granulated sugar into a saucepan over moderate heat. Stir and, when the sugar is dissolved, raise the heat and bring to

the boil. Add the apricots, lower the heat and simmer until the apricots are tender. Remove 12 apricot halves, put them in a bowl and set aside to cool. When they are cool, cover and refrigerate.

Sieve the remaining apricots and return the purée to the pan. Cook over low heat until it is thick. Remove from the heat and mix in the kirsch. Cool, cover and refrigerate.

Shortly before serving take the rice out of the refrigerator. Carefully run a knife around the edge of the soufflé dish or mould and turn the pudding out on to a serving dish. Arrange the reserved apricots on top, pour the sauce over the fruit and serve.

If you wish to serve the pudding hot, place the cooked rice in a fireproof serving dish. Arrange the apricots on top of the rice and decorate with glacé cherries and angelica. Put the dish back in the oven and heat thoroughly. Serve the sauce separately in a small jug.

Cheese Soufflé

A perfect soufflé is generally considered to be a tricky temperamental dish to make, but this recipe for Cheese Soufflé is very easy to prepare. It is advisable to serve the soufflé as soon as it is cooked, otherwise it will sink. Serve it with a crisp green salad, or a green vegetable such as courgettes [zucchini] and French bread or serve it with sliced raw tomatoes for an interesting colour contrast.

6-8 SERVINGS

2 oz. [$\frac{1}{4}$ cup] plus 1 tablespoon butter
5 oz. [1$\frac{1}{4}$ cups] cheese, coarsely grated (preferably a mixture of Gruyere and Parmesan)
4 tablespoons flour
10 fl. oz. [1$\frac{1}{4}$ cups] milk, scalded
1 teaspoon salt
$\frac{1}{8}$ teaspoon white pepper
$\frac{1}{8}$ teaspoon ground mace
$\frac{1}{8}$ teaspoon paprika
5 egg yolks
6 egg whites
$\frac{1}{4}$ teaspoon cream of tartar

Preheat the oven to moderate 350°F (Gas Mark 4, 180°C).

With the tablespoon of butter, grease a 2$\frac{1}{2}$-pint [6$\frac{1}{4}$ cup] soufflé dish. Sprinkle 4 tablespoons of the grated cheese around the inside of the dish and, with a table knife, press it on to the bottom and sides. Set the soufflé dish aside.

In a large saucepan, melt the remaining butter over moderate heat. With a wooden spoon, stir the flour into the butter and cook, stirring constantly, for 1 minute. Do not let this roux brown.

Remove the pan from the heat. Gradually add the milk, stirring constantly.

Return the pan to the heat and cook the mixture, stirring constantly, for 1 minute or until it is thick and smooth.

Remove the pan from the heat and add $\frac{1}{2}$ teaspoon salt, the pepper, mace and paprika. Beat the egg yolks, a little at a time, into the hot sauce. Set the pan aside to allow the egg yolk mixture to cool slightly.

In a mixing bowl, beat the egg whites with a rotary beater or wire whisk until they are foamy. Add the remaining salt and the cream of tartar. Continue beating until the egg whites form stiff peaks.

Stir the remaining cheese into the hot sauce. When the cheese is thoroughly mixed in, spoon the egg whites on top of the sauce and gently, but quickly, fold them in with a metal spoon.

Spoon the mixture into the prepared soufflé dish. With a table knife, carefully mark a deep circle in the centre of the soufflé.

Place the soufflé in the centre of the oven and bake for 40 to 45 minutes, or until it is lightly brown on top and it has risen $\frac{1}{2}$ inch above the top of the dish. Remove the soufflé dish from the oven and serve at once.

Cooking with Nuts and Fruit

Fruit and nuts originally formed the basic ingredients in man's diet. But during the Early Roman Empire, they were regarded more as a delicacy to be served as desserts. In Greece it was a custom to greet guests with a small plate of glazed fruit or nuts, accompanied by a glass of water. This tradition continues in the Western world today, when olives and salted nuts are served with aperitifs.

With the advantages of modern transportation and preservation, most nuts and fruit are available throughout the world, although they are possibly not used to their full potential. Fruit is essential to our everyday diet, chiefly for its high vitamin content; nuts are a valuable source of protein.

Citrus fruits; apples and pears, peaches and apricots tend to be taken for granted. We usually eat them fresh and succulent without much thought as to how their particular flavours can be used to enhance meat and fish dishes and everyday cooking.

Nuts and fruit incorporated into your everyday cooking add an exciting and interesting taste to your meals.

Softer fruit, which includes strawberries, raspberries, bilberries, blackcurrants and blueberries are more seasonal, but modern canning and freezing methods ensure their availability throughout the year. These fruits are superb as desserts and preserves. They combine with savoury ingredients to make unusual salads and sauces. Their purées blended with cream produce ices and soufflés. The whole fruit, chopped fruit, or the fine slivers of orange or lemon peel make attractive garnishes for savoury dishes, as well as decorating flans and cakes. Glacé fruit such as cherries or grapefruit is delicious to eat by itself as well as being an attractive decoration.

Plums, grapes and cherries can also be used in desserts or salads. Avocado pears and melons may be used as hors-d'oeuvres. More exotic fruit such as mangoes, lychees and pomegranates can add an unusual taste and colour to many dishes. Do not forget the tomato and olive which are recognized fruits, although they are generally used in a similar way to vegetables.

Nuts are as versatile as fruit and come in varieties such as: Brazil, walnut, chestnut, almond, pistachio, cashew, pine nut, pecan, Macadamia, peanut and coconut.

Nuts may be used as a substitute for meat, as in the case of many vegetarian dishes. They are also suitable to add to soups, sauces, stuffings and soufflés. Nuts, whether ground, chopped, or cut into slivers can make attractive garnishes and tasty sweetmeats. Chopped nuts, for example, fried with onions make a delicious garnish for meat, fish, or vegetables. Nuts can be used in cakes and bread, and as butter fillings for sandwiches. To decorate a cake, lightly sprinkle chopped roasted nuts or desiccated coconut over it.

There are many more varieties of nuts and fruit although names may differ depending on the locality. With a little forethought and imagination you can include this wide variety of nuts and fruit in your daily diet.

Stewing or Poaching Fruit

Apples, pears, apricots, plums and blackcurrants are some fruits which often need pre-cooking before they are used in recipes. Poaching may be done on the top of the stove using a heavy pan with a lid, or in the oven in a casserole.

To make a compote of whole fruit, it is essential to use the following guidelines. Use 1 lb. fruit to $\frac{1}{2}$ pint [$2\frac{1}{2}$ cups] water and 4 oz. [$\frac{1}{2}$ cup] sugar. The fruit should be prepared by stoning apricots and plums, or peeling and coring apples and pears. Then dissolve the sugar in the water and boil the syrup rapidly for at least 2 minutes before adding the fruit. The halves or quarters of the prepared fruit may now be added to the syrup and simmered gently in a covered pan for 10 to 15 minutes or until tender.

To obtain a purée, the sugar should be added only after the cooking. Less water is needed—$\frac{1}{4}$ to $\frac{1}{2}$ inch is enough. The fruit should be cooked more rapidly with continual stirring, until it is reduced to a pulp. Finer purées may be obtained by pushing the cooked pulp through a sieve, or using a blender. Then add the sugar and the purée is ready for use as a basis for sauces, cakes or pies. Cloves, cinnamon, lemon rind or wine added to the sugar syrup—each gives a subtle flavour to the compote or purée.

Dried fruit may be prepared in much the same way as fresh fruit, although it requires soaking in water for a period of 12 hours before being cooked. Use $\frac{1}{2}$ lb. fruit soaked in 1 pint [$2\frac{1}{2}$ cups] water. Simmer gently until the fruit is tender, and add 2 to 4 oz. [$\frac{1}{4}$ to $\frac{1}{2}$ cup] sugar. Simmer the fruit for a further 5 minutes. Dried fruit includes prunes, apricots,

figs and peaches. Currants, raisins and sultanas need no preparation or cooking. They are ideal for cake making, sauces and stuffings.

Roasting, Salting and Blanching Nuts
Most nuts become far more digestible once they have been roasted, and their flavours are certainly improved.

Shelled or whole nuts may be placed on a baking tray and left in the oven at 275°F, Gas Mark 1, 140°C for 30 minutes, turning occasionally. Once roasted, remove the shells as for chestnuts, or rub off the skins as for almonds or hazelnuts. Commercial roasting is often done with hot sand as this gives a more uniform heat.

To blanch nuts remove the skin by immersing the nuts in boiling water for a few minutes. Drain and rub them between your thumb and forefinger. The skin of almonds or pistachios comes away easily and the nuts should then be thoroughly dried before use.

Blanched nuts may be fried for 5 minutes in a little vegetable oil until crisp and brown. Then drain them and toss them in salt and pepper—cayenne pepper gives a spicy flavour. Cover the nuts and leave them in a warm place to dry.

MENUS

* asterisk indicates recipe is given.

SUNDAY
Breakfast
Orange juice
Bacon and tomatoes
Toast and marmalade
Tea or coffee

Lunch
Cream cheese and pineapple salad
Slice of buttered nut bread*
Tea or coffee

Dinner
Tomato juice
Roast chicken with raisin and almond stuffing
Peas and baked tomatoes
Potato croquettes
Gooseberry soufflé

MONDAY
Breakfast
Swiss-style Muesli
Bacon and mushrooms
Toast
Tea or coffee

Lunch
Hawaiian risotto*
Fresh fruit ice-cream
Tea or coffee

Dinner
Cranberry soup*
Pork cutlets with quince
Sliced green beans and carrots
Raspberry condé

TUESDAY
Breakfast
Prunes
Boiled or poached egg
Toast
Tea or coffee

Lunch
Nut roast and salad*
Fresh fruit fool
Tea or coffee

Dinner
Grapefruit juice
Baked stuffed plaice or flounder
Peas and beans with almond and onion topping
Hazelnut meringues

WEDNESDAY
Breakfast
Cereal with fruit
Scrambled egg and bacon
Toast
Tea or coffee

Lunch
Hamburger and salad
Fruit fritters and cream
Tea or coffee

Dinner
Melon cocktail
Chicken and pineapple
Baked bananas
Tomatoes and peas
Blackcurrant crunch*

THURSDAY
Breakfast
Lemon juice
Apple potato cake and bacon
Toast
Tea or coffee

Lunch
Grapefruit and shellfish salad
Yogurt
Tea or coffee

Dinner
Dressed avocado
Braised liver and carrots
Duchesse potatoes
Fruit surprise*

FRIDAY
Breakfast
½ grilled [broiled] grapefruit
Boiled or poached egg
Toast
Tea or coffee

Lunch
Ham savour*
Peach sherbert
Tea or coffee

Dinner
Nut soup*
Lamb chops in orange sauce
Crunchy buttered cabbage with baked tomatoes
Cherry almond flan*

SATURDAY
Breakfast
Pineapple juice
Smoked haddock
Toast
Tea or coffee

Lunch
Cottage cheese, pineapple and
mixed nut salad
Spiced pears and cream with fruit
and nut topping
Tea or coffee

Dinner
Tomato juice
Sausages with apple and raisin sauce*
Spaghetti and savoury nut topping
Fresh fruit salad

RECIPES

Nut bread
2 cups self-raising flour
1 cup milk
1 cup sugar
1 cup chopped nuts

Preheat the oven to 375°F, Gas Mark 5,
190°C.
Use a small teacup to measure all the
ingredients. Put them in a bowl and mix
to a smooth consistency. Pour the mixture into a greased 1 lb. loaf tin. Bake in
the oven for 45 minutes. Any nuts may
be used, but 1 cup of mixed fruit may be
substituted for the nuts.

Hawaiian Risotto
1 oz. [2 tablespoons] **margarine**
1 onion, chopped
8 medium-sized mushrooms,
chopped
3 slices bacon, chopped
6 oz. [2½ cups] **cooked long grain
rice**
½ lb. [1½ cups] **cooked pork, chicken
or beef, diced**
2 tomatoes, skinned and chopped
2 tablespoons canned corn
2 tablespoons cooked peas
2 oz. pineapple, chopped

Melt the fat in a large frying pan. Gently
fry the chopped onion, mushrooms and
bacon for 5 minutes. Add the rice and
cooked meat and gently mix well together. Heat for about 10 minutes,
stirring frequently. Mix in the tomatoes,
corn, peas and pineapple and remove
from the heat after 5 minutes. Serve hot.

Cranberry Soup
½ lb. **cranberries**
1½ pints [3¾ cups] **water**
lemon rind
2 oz. [¼ cup] **sugar**
1 teaspoon cornflour [cornstarch]

Prepare the fruit and place in a pan with
the water, lemon rind and sugar. Bring
to the boil and simmer for 20 minutes.
Rub through a sieve or use a blender,
straining afterwards.

Mix the cornflour [cornstarch] in a
little water to make a smooth paste and
add to the mixture. Stir over a steady
heat until the soup thickens. Add a small
glass of wine to flavour the soup.
Cherries, plums or currants may be
used as a variation.

Nut Roast
4 oz. [2 cups] **fresh breadcrumbs**
4 oz. [1 cup] **chopped nuts**
1 small onion, grated
2 tomatoes, skinned and sliced
¼ pint [⅝ cup] **milk**
1 egg
salt and pepper

Preheat the oven to 350°F, Gas Mark 4,
180°C.
Mix together the breadcrumbs, nuts,
onions, tomatoes and seasoning. Beat the
egg into the milk and add to the mixture.
Press into a baking tin and bake in the
oven for 30 minutes. Serve cold.

Blackcurrant Crunch
4 oz. shortcrust pastry
1 pint [2½ cups] **fruit purée**
2 oz. [¼ cup] **margarine**
2 oz. [½ cup] **flour**
2 oz. [¼ cup] **sugar**
1 oz. [¼ cup] **chopped nuts**

Preheat the oven to 400°F, Gas Mark 6,
200°C.
Line an 8-inch pie dish with the pastry.
Pour the fruit purée into the dish.
Rub the fat into the flour and add the
sugar and nuts. Sprinkle this over the top
of the fruit and bake in the oven for 25
to 30 minutes. Serve hot.

Fruit Surprise
1 lb. mixed fruit—apples and
blackberries; strawberries and
raspberries; peaches and apricots
1 pint [2½ cups] **water**
6 oz. [¾ cup] **sugar**
grated rind and juice of 1 lemon
3 tablespoons cornflour [cornstarch]

Prepare and clean the fruit. Simmer in
half the water until tender. Pass through
a sieve and purée the fruit. Make this up
to 1 pint [2½ cups] with the rest of the
water and add sugar and lemon.
Mix the cornflour [cornstarch] with a
little water to make a smooth paste. Add
this to the mixture and bring to the boil
stirring all the time until it thickens.
When cool, place in a serving bowl and
decorate with whipped cream and fruit.

Ham Savour
4 slices cooked ham
4 pineapple 'fingers' or bananas
1 oz. [2 tablespoons] **butter**
1 oz. [¼ cup] **flour**
½ pint [1¼ cups] **milk**
4 oz. [1 cup] **grated cheese**
salt and pepper

Preheat the oven to 350°F, Gas Mark 4,
180°C.

Roll the ham around the fruit and place
these rolls in a heatproof dish.
Make a cheese sauce by melting the
butter and adding the flour. Cook gently.
Add the milk, stirring until the mixture
has thickened. Remove from the heat and
add the cheese and seasoning. Pour over
the rolls and sprinkle with grated cheese.
Bake in the oven for 15 to 20 minutes.

Nut Soup
1 small onion, chopped
2 celery sticks, chopped
1 oz. [2 tablespoons] **butter**
2 pints [5 cups] **chicken stock**
4 oz. [1 cup] **chopped nuts—
almonds, hazelnuts and walnuts**
1 oz. [¼ cup] **cornflour [cornstarch]**
1 tablespoon tomato purée
¼ pint [⅝ cup] **milk**
salt and pepper

Lightly fry the onion and celery in the
butter until soft. Add the nuts, stock and
seasoning. Simmer gently for 30 minutes.
Pass through a sieve or blender, then
return to the pan.
Mix the cornflour [cornstarch] with a
little water to make a smooth paste. Add
the cornflour paste, tomato purée and
milk to the nut mixture. Bring to the boil
stirring all the time. Cook for 3 minutes.

Cherry Almond Flan
4 oz. [½ cup] **margarine**
4 oz. [½ cup] **sugar**
2 eggs, beaten
3 oz. [¾ cup] **self-raising flour**
2 oz. [⅓ cup] **ground almonds**
compote of cherries thickened
with a little arrowroot or
cornflour [cornstarch]

Preheat the oven to 375°F, Gas Mark 5,
190°C.
Cream together the fat and the sugar,
then add the beaten eggs half at a time.
Fold in the sifted flour and ground
almonds. Place in a greased sandwich or
flan tin seven inches in diameter.
Bake in the oven for 20 to 25 minutes.
When cool, fill the centre with the compote. Decorate with flaked almonds.

Sausages with Apple and Raisin
Sauce
1 lb. pork sausages
½ pint [1¼ cups] **water**
2 oz. [⅓ cup] **raisins**
1 tablespoon apple sauce
2 teaspoons cornflour [cornstarch]
brown sugar and lemon juice

Put the water, raisins and apple sauce in
a pan and simmer for 7 minutes. Mean-
while, gently fry or grill [broil] the
sausages. Mix the cornflour [cornstarch]
with a little water to make a paste. Add
this to the sauce and stir until it has
thickened. Stir in the sugar and lemon
juice to taste. Place the sausages on a bed
of cooked spaghetti tossed in a fried
onion and nut mixture. Pour the sauce
over the top and serve immediately.

The Magic of Garlic and Onions

Onions and garlic are two of the greatest and most versatile natural flavouring agents in the world. Yet many people still tend to regard them with a considerable amount of suspicion and use them sparingly or rarely in their cooking.

This love-hate relationship with onions and garlic seems to stem, at least in part, from the reputation they have for adding an overwhelming flavour to food and leaving a lingering smell on the breath and in the room in which they are cooked. However, far from masking the flavours of food, onions and garlic can actually help to enhance and intensify them. They can add either a subtle or a pungent flavour to the food; it all depends on the amount you use.

The taste for onions and garlic, as for other seasonings, is very much a matter of personal taste. If you are not used to either onions or garlic, it is always wise to be prudent rather than lavish with the amount you use, at least until you are familiar with the dish or know how much of an oniony or garlicky taste you, your family and your friends enjoy.

The trouble is, many people do not know what delicious flavours they are missing when they omit what they consider the foreign flavour of onions and garlic from their food. However, you cannot really tell people how marvellous onions and garlic are. They have to

experience the flavours for themselves to really appreciate them. If in the past you have been rather cautious in your use of garlic and onions, you might be pleasantly surprised by adopting a slightly more adventurous attitude to them. The ideas and recipes that follow provide an excellent introduction to the versatility of these flavouring agents. Try some of them and find out what a difference even a little onion or garlic can make to the simplest of dishes.

GARLIC

Over the centuries garlic has been credited with magical and health-giving powers. It has antiseptic properties, containing an antibiotic called allicin. It is considered good for the digestion and will ease coughs and colds.

The bulb of the garlic is made up of a collection of individual segments or cloves and the whole is covered by a white, mauve or pink papery outer skin. Recipes generally advise using a clove of garlic, but before you can use the clove, the husk surrounding it needs to be peeled off.

A whole clove of garlic can give piquancy to a sauce, soup, stew or casserole but do remember to remove it before serving the dish. A clove dropped into French dressing, not more than 24 hours before serving, will add zest to

your salad. For a lighter touch, rub a cut clove around an empty salad bowl.

Slivers of garlic pushed into a leg of lamb near the bone add flavour to your roast. Or put a clove or two under the meat in your roasting pan where it will add relish to both the meat and the gravy without being overwhelming.

A quick and easy way to give a light garlic flavour to bread is by rubbing the outside of a French loaf with a cut clove and then heating the bread in the oven at about 350°F, Gas Mark 4, 180°C, until it is crisp. Serve it hot straight from the oven.

A more elaborate method of making garlic bread is to spread a mixture of two crushed cloves of garlic, a teaspoon of chopped parsley, a pinch of salt and about 3 to 4 ounces [½ cup] of butter on a French loaf which you have cut into slices almost all the way through, leaving the bottom crust intact. Wrap the loaf in aluminium foil and put it in a preheated oven at 350°F, Gas Mark 4, 180°C, for about 15 minutes.

When a recipe calls for crushed garlic you can press out the juices with the flat blade of a knife on a wooden board, with the back of a spoon against the side of a small bowl, with a pestle and mortar, or in a garlic press. Use just the juice and a little flesh, discarding any fibrous matter. The juice of a crushed clove enhances

marinades, poultry, beef and lamb dishes and vegetable dishes such as aubergines [eggplants], courgettes [zucchini], sweet peppers, ratatouille and piperade.

Never allow garlic to brown as it develops a bitter taste. When you are cooking onions and garlic together it is best to sauté the onions first and then add the garlic. If you are preparing a dish to be frozen and kept in the deep-freeze, omit the garlic from the dish and add it when you are heating the food as garlic tends to develop a musty flavour when it is deep frozen. Old, stale garlic also imparts a heavy, slightly musty flavour to food.

There are dehydrated forms of garlic that do not leave a smell on the hands as their flavour is only released when they are moistened. The equivalent quantities are usually given on the jar or packet but, in general, dehydrated products are more concentrated than the fresh. For example, one-eighth of a teaspoon of garlic powder is equal to one clove of fresh garlic. It is always wise to read the instructions before use.

Garlic powder can be used for any recipe calling for fresh garlic, such as savoury butters, soups, stews, marinades and sauces.

Garlic salt (garlic powder with salt added) adds a piquancy to salads, omelettes, canapés, spaghetti, meat and poultry dishes, and enhances the flavour of grilled [broiled] or fried foods. However, you will need to use less salt than the recipe calls for.

Garlic spread is a concentrated paste which can be used to add zest to grilled [broiled] and roast meat and baked potatoes and vegetables; blend it with margarine or butter and add just before serving. It is ideal for garlic bread.

ONIONS
Onions contain a number of nutrients— small amounts of protein, carbohydrate, iron, iodine, the B vitamins and vitamin C, as well as sulphur. The presence of sulphur in onions causes digestive upsets in some people: it is also the compound which causes any silver to tarnish upon contact with it.

There are several varieties of onions— countries with a warm climate, such as Spain, produce a large onion with a milder flavour; the countries with cooler climates, such as Britain, produce onions with a stronger flavour and better keeping qualities. The colour ranges from silver-white through yellow to a purplish-red: the white onions tend to be milder than the yellow or purplish-red varieties. The shape is as varied as the flavour and colour; it can be oval and flat, large and round, small and round, medium-sized and globe-shaped. Onions are available all the year round.

Button or pickling onions are small and round with brown skins and white flesh. They are harvested before they are fully matured and used for pickling or in cooking as a garnish. They tend to be too strong to eat raw.

Silver-skinned onions are small with white flesh and a silver skin and much prized for pickling. These are also too strong to eat raw.

All-purpose onions are medium in size and slightly squat in shape. They have a strong flavour and may be dark skinned or pale golden.

Spanish [Bermuda] onions are very large, with a glossy brown skin and mild flavour. They are ideal for boiling, braising or roasting and sweet enough to eat raw. In America, the term refers to any imported variety.

Racambole onions bear 'fruit' at the top of their stems and look like shallots. They have a garlicky flavour and are also called Spanish garlic.

Spring onions [scallions] are often the thinnings of the main crop of onion. Both the green spears and the white bulb are edible and can be used raw in salads or as a garnish for soups. You can sharpen an omelette or a salad dressing with the addition of a few finely-chopped raw spring onions [scallions].

Shallots are small, tender and delicate in flavour with a white bulb. They are principally salad onions, but can be used in cooking and are particularly useful when only a faint flavour of onion is required.

Preparation without tears
As much as you may enjoy the flavour of onions, they are a bane when it comes to preparing and chopping them. To prevent tears you can skin them under cold running water. Slice the peeled onions with a very sharp knife almost through to the roots in thin layers and then slice them again at right angles to the original cuts. They will fall into neat pieces. It helps to do all this preparation near cold running water which disperses the volatile substances that cause the eyes to smart and water.

Removing the aftermath
To remove a strong oniony or garlicky smell from your hands after preparation rub your hands well with salt, vinegar or lemon juice and then rinse them thoroughly under cold running water. If you have been eating onions and do not want the smell to linger on your breath, chew a piece of fresh parsley to help neutralize the aftertaste.

Choosing and storing

Look for onions which are firm with feathery paper skins and no hint of growth either at the root or at the top. Avoid buying onions which are discoloured, soft or with a green growth tip showing, as this means they are old stock. Store onions in a cool, dry, airy place.

Methods of cooking onions

Onions are a versatile vegetable in their own right as well as invaluable for adding a rich, robust flavour to soups, sauces, pies, stews and casseroles.

Braised onions—choose a large Spanish [Bermuda] onion. Remove the outer skin and trim the root. Pack them close together in a deep, ovenproof casserole. Place some chopped fatty bacon between each onion. Season with salt and pepper. Add 2 tablespoons of water or stock. Cover tightly and cook in the oven at 400°F, Gas Mark 6, 200°C, for about 1½ hours until tender.

Baked onions—wash some medium-sized Spanish [Bermuda] onions but do not peel them. Wrap each onion in aluminium foil and stand them on a baking tray. Cook in the oven at 350°F, Gas Mark 4, 180°C, for about 60 minutes or until soft when squeezed. When cooked, slice off the root end and top and remove the skin. Serve very hot with melted butter.

Boiled onions — choose even-sized Spanish [Bermuda] onions. Remove the brown outer skin and trim the root. Place the onions in boiling salted water and boil gently for 45 to 60 minutes, depending on the size, until tender. Drain carefully and use the liquid to make a sauce to serve with the onions.

Crispy fried onion rings — choose Spanish [Bermuda] onions. Remove the brown outer skin and slice. Dip the rings into seasoned flour and then in milk and then into the flour again; or dip in a batter mixture. Drop the coated rings in hot oil and fry until crisp and golden. Drain on kitchen paper. Use as a garnish for grilled [broiled] meat or fish.

Roasted onions — remove the outer brown skin and cook the onions in a little fat in the oven at 400°F, Gas Mark 6, 200°C for about 60 minutes until tender. Or bake them with roasting meat.

Sautéed onions — remove the brown outer skin and cut into very thin slices. Melt some fat in a frying pan, add the onion rings and sauté gently until they are golden brown, stirring frequently to prevent them from burning. Season with salt. Sautéed onions are a tasty garnish for pale soups, grills and liver.

Stewed onions — choose even-sized Spanish [Bermuda] onions. Remove the brown outer skin. Stew them in a little milk, seasoned with a peppercorn and clove to each onion, for 45 to 60 minutes until tender. Remove them carefully and use the milky liquid to make a sauce to serve with the onions. They are delicious with roast and boiled lamb, boiled chicken, ham and pork.

Instant onions are a marvellous standby for giving that professional touch to dishes when guests arrive unexpectedly. Traditional Welsh rarebit can be given extra piquancy with the addition of dehydrated onions. They are not strong enough for use in stews.

Salad onion flakes are excellent for garnishing both cold and hot foods, as they are a mixture of green, red and white flakes and crisp in texture. They need to be covered with cold water and soaked for 10 minutes before using. For a really crisp texture use iced water or refrigerate.

Onion salt is a quick way of adding zest to all meat, fish and poultry dishes, soups, sauces and gravies. It is concentrated, so use sparingly. You will also need to use less salt than given in the recipe.

Minced onion and onion flakes require reconstituting in cold water and can then be used as for fresh onions in soups and stews, stuffing mixtures, beefburgers, meat patties and sauces and gravies.

Recipes

FISH PIPERADE
This very easy dish is suitable for a dinner or lunch-time party.
SERVES 4
- 1 tablespoon cooking oil
- 2 medium-sized onions, peeled and chopped
- 2 medium-sized green peppers, deseeded and chopped
- 2 tomatoes, peeled and chopped
- 2 cloves garlic, crushed
  salt and pepper to taste
- 1 lb. cod or haddock fillets
  chopped parsley for garnish

Preheat the oven to 350°F, Gas Mark 4, 180°C.

Heat the oil in a frying pan and add the onions and peppers. Cook gently for about 10 minutes until soft. Add the tomatoes, garlic, salt and pepper and cook for a further 15 minutes.

Place the fish in a greased ovenproof dish and cover with the vegetable mixture. Cook in the oven for 20 to 30 minutes until the fish is tender. Garnish with parsley and serve immediately.

ONION AND EGG PIE
This is a tasty lunch-time or supper dish which can be prepared the day before.
SERVES 4
- 2 tablespoons cooking oil
- 4 medium-sized onions, peeled and chopped
- 4 eggs, hard-boiled and sliced
  salt and pepper to taste
- 2 tablespoons butter
- 2 tablespoons cornflour [cornstarch]
- ½ pint [1¼ cups] milk
- 2 oz. [¼ cup] margarine or butter
- 4 oz. [2 cups] fresh breadcrumbs

Preheat the oven to 375°F, Gas Mark 5, 190°C.

Heat the oil in a frying pan, add the onions and sauté gently until they are soft and golden. Place the sliced eggs and onions in alternate layers in a greased ovenproof casserole. Lightly season each layer.

Make the white sauce by melting the butter in a pan. Mix in the cornflour [cornstarch] to make a paste. Gradually stir in the milk. Cook gently until the sauce is thick and smooth. Pour the white sauce over the eggs and onions.

Melt the margarine or butter in a pan and stir in the breadcrumbs until all the fat is absorbed. Spread the breadcrumbs on top of the onion and egg mixture. Bake in the oven for 30 to 45 minutes until the mixture is bubbling and the crumbs are crisp.

ONION AND KIDNEY CASSEROLE
This is a rich and nutritious dish for a cold winter's evening.
SERVES 4
- 4 pigs' kidneys, cut into small pieces and tossed in seasoned flour
- 2 tablespoons cooking oil
- 1 large onion, peeled and chopped
- 1 cooking apple, peeled and chopped
- 1 tablespoon chopped parsley
- 1 teaspoon sage
  stock or water

Preheat the oven to 325°F, Gas Mark 3, 170°C.

Heat the oil and sauté the onion gently until transparent. Add the kidney and apple and sauté lightly. Turn into an ovenproof dish with herbs, stock or water. Cook in the oven for 1½ to 2 hours. Adjust seasoning to taste. Serve with rice.

ONION AND TOMATO CHARLOTTE
This dish is good hot or cold and is a savoury accompaniment to any meat dish.
SERVES 4—6
- 3 tablespoons cooking oil
- 1 lb. onions, peeled and sliced
- 1 teaspoon yeast extract
- ¼ teaspoon basil or mixed herbs
- 1 tablespoon chopped parsley
- 2 cloves garlic, crushed
- 14 oz. canned tomatoes
  salt and pepper to taste
- 2 oz. [¼ cup] margarine or butter
- 4 oz. [2 cups] fresh breadcrumbs

Preheat the oven to 375°F, Gas Mark 5, 190°C.

Heat the oil in a frying pan. Add the onions, cover the pan and cook over a low heat for about 20 minutes until pale yellow. Stir in the yeast extract, basil or mixed herbs, parsley, garlic and tomatoes. Adjust the seasoning to taste. Turn into a greased ovenproof casserole.

Melt the margarine or butter in the pan and stir in the breadcrumbs until all the fat is absorbed. Spread the breadcrumbs on top of the onion and tomato mixture. Bake in the oven for about 45 minutes until the crumbs are crisp.

ONIONS A LA GRECQUE

Serve this dish as an hors-d'oeuvre or as a salad with cold meats. The addition of the parsley will help to reduce any oniony aftertaste and odours.

SERVES 4

  2 tablespoons cooking oil
  8 oz. button onions, peeled and
    blanched for 5 minutes
  1 tablespoon wine vinegar
  3-4 tomatoes, skinned and finely
    chopped
    bouquet garni
  1 clove garlic, crushed
    salt and pepper to taste
  2 tablespoons chopped parsley

Put the olive oil, blanched onions, wine vinegar, tomatoes, bouquet garni, garlic, salt and pepper into a pan. Cover and simmer for about 40 minutes—the onions should be tender but still whole.

  Gently remove the onions to a dish. Stir the parsley into the mixture remaining in the pan. Pour over the onions and leave to cool. This dish should be served cold but not chilled. To avoid chilling, store on a low refrigerator shelf.

ONION AND APPLE SAUCE

This piquant sauce is an excellent complement for roast pork, sausages, goose, duck and pheasant.

  2 oz. [$\frac{1}{4}$ cup] butter
  1 lb. onions, peeled and finely
    chopped
  1 lb. cooking apples, peeled and
    finely chopped
  1 tablespoon soft brown sugar
    pinch of salt
  $\frac{1}{4}$ pint [$\frac{5}{8}$ cup] sweet cooking sherry
    or sweet white wine

Melt the butter in a pan. Add the onions and apples, sugar and salt. Cover and simmer gently until the onions and apples are tender and the mixture is the consistency of a thick soup. Stir occasionally to prevent sticking. Beat well and add the sherry or white wine. Turn into a bowl to serve.

ONION AND BEETROOT [BEET] SALAD

This zesty salad is a splendid complement for cold ham or tongue.

SERVES 4

  3 medium-sized boiled beetroots
    [beets], peeled and sliced
  1 large Spanish [Bermuda] onion,
    peeled and finely sliced
  1 tablespoon chopped parsley

FRENCH DRESSING:

  3 tablespoons salad oil
  1 tablespoon wine or garlic vinegar
  $\frac{1}{4}$ teaspoon dry mustard
    salt and pepper to taste

Place alternate layers of beetroot [beet], onion and a light sprinkling of parsley in a salad bowl.

  Blend all the ingredients for the French dressing together, stirring well, and pour over the salad.

Is milk good for you?

Milk and its by-products play a nutritionally important role in our daily lives. A tall glass of refreshingly cool milk, dairy ice-cream topped with fresh fruit, a cheese-board with an enticing selection of cheeses for a buffet party—these are not only tasty, they are also good for you. Even if you do not consider yourself 'a great milk drinker' and prefer your coffee or tea without milk, no doubt you have some milk in your refrigerator which you use to make a cheese sauce or to thicken a soup. People who eat yogurts to help themselves lose weight, maybe without realizing it, are obtaining all the important nutrients from a milk product.

One pint or one quart of milk contains one-sixth of your daily need for the nutrients that are most important for good health. On average, one pint or one quart of pasteurized milk contains: 360 Calories, or more depending on the amount of butterfat; 18 grams of protein; 680 milligrams of calcium; 0.4 milligrams of iron; 258 micrograms of vitamin A—217 in the winter; 0.2 milligrams of thiamin; 0.85 milligrams of riboflavin; 5.2 milligrams of nicotinic acid equivalents; 8.5 milligrams of vitamin C—but this decreases when stored; 0.29 micrograms of vitamin D are found in summer and in winter 0.06 micrograms. By weight, milk is 87 per cent water. Any heat-treated milk is lower in vitamin C, iron and carbohydrates, but you can get these respectively from citrus fruit, liver and kidneys and bread.

Research has proved that these nutrients contribute to your general health. Vitamin A keeps skin and eyes healthy; the B complex which includes thiamin and B_{12} improves digestion, helps to convert carbohydrates into energy and is good for the heart and nervous system. Riboflavin (vitamin B_1) keeps the skin and the mucous membranes in good condition and helps the body cells to make the most effective use of oxygen. Nicotinic acid or niacin nourishes the skin. It aids growth and is also important in metabolizing food into energy. Vitamin D enables the body to make good use of the plentiful calcium in milk which is vital for strong teeth and bones. Vitamin C prevents certain skin diseases and helps to speed recovery from infections, and keeps gums, muscles and bones healthy.

It does not follow, however, that by drinking six pints [three quarts] of milk a day you will be living on a perfect diet. As milk does not contain all the nutrients the body needs in sufficient quantities, it must be supplemented by other food to give maximum nourishment.

Methods of grading milk vary from country to country. In the United Kingdom fresh cows' milk is divided into four main categories: untreated, pasteurized, UHT (ultra heat treated) and sterilized milk. Within these grades other kinds are found: homogenized milk, Channel Island milk from Jersey and Guernsey herds and South Devon milk—the last two have a minimum of four per cent butterfat. This can be discerned at a glance because the cream at the top is yellow.

The most nutritional benefits from milk are to be obtained from untreated milk which must come from specially licensed farms and dairies. Untreated, or raw, milk is not subjected to any form of heat treatment. Although rigid tests and controls are applied in most Western countries to make milk safe for human consumption, there is a slight possibility of brucellosis (undulant fever) being

By including milk in your daily diet you can enhance your beauty as well as protect your general health.

passed on if the milk is not heat treated. Other milk-borne diseases such as diphtheria, typhoid fever, gastro-enteritis, dysentry and a septic sore throat, but excluding tuberculosis and brucellosis, can also be caused by the careless handling of milk, contaminated water or utensils used during the processing of milk. Although cows are susceptible to tuberculosis which can then be passed on to human beings, most Western countries enforce very strict tests, controls and regulations pertaining to the production of milk and outbreaks of disease are now extremely rare.

The heating process of pasteurization destroys milk-borne bacteria and does not significantly affect the nutritional value of milk. The milk is heated to 145°F (63°C) for half an hour, or heated to not less than 161°F (72°C) for 15 seconds. The milk is cooled rapidly to prevent growth of heat-resistant organisms and the decrease of nutritional value. Pasteurized milk is sometimes homogenized. Homogenized milk is heat treated and processed so that fat globules are evenly distributed throughout and a 'cream line' is not formed. Homogenized milk has a smooth creamy taste and is readily digested because of the smaller fat globules.

Ultra heat treated milk is subjected to very intense heat of 270°F (132°C) for one second. Packed under sterile conditions, ultra heat treated milk keeps without refrigeration if unopened for up to three weeks and stays 'fresh' for several months when refrigerated in sealed aluminium containers, although the flavour will gradually deteriorate.

Sterilized milk is heated to temperatures of up to 230°F (110°C) which destroy all bacteria and micro-organisms. Sterilized milk tastes and looks rather like boiled milk with a creamy appearance but it will keep unrefrigerated for up to about three months as long as it is unopened.

Skimmed milk is made by removing the fat from fresh milk and so loses the fat-soluble vitamins such as A and D but retains the proteins, carbohydrate, vitamin C and water. Another low-fat milk is buttermilk, the liquid residue from butter manufacture. It can be either sweet or sour depending on which cream has been used and is much the same as skimmed milk in food value.

Filled milk is a mixture of skimmed milk and vegetable fats for people on special diets. Whey is the watery liquid left after the milk curd has been separated during cheese manufacture and it contains a relatively large percentage of lactose—milk sugar—and riboflavin.

Milk is sold in many forms: dried, canned and frozen. Each one has a slight difference in the percentage of the various nutrients.

There are six grades of dried milk: full, three-quarter; half and quarter cream; partly skimmed and skimmed. Dried full milk powder is made from homogenized milk so it contains all the fat. The processes used in drying preserve the proteins. Generally, powdered milk is easily reconstituted with water. The fat content of dried milk varies from 26 per cent in the full cream milk powder to less than 1.5 per cent in the dried skimmed milk. The quantities of thiamin, vitamin B_{12} and vitamin C are only slightly diminished. Dried skimmed milk contains almost no fat—therefore no vitamins A and D, although it is often fortified with these vitamins—but it retains the proteins, calcium and riboflavin of fresh milk.

Evaporated milk is unsweetened condensed full- or half-cream milk whereas sweetened condensed milk has about 15 per cent cane sugar added. The sugar helps to preserve the milk so high temperature sterilization in canning is unnecessary.

Say Cheese!

Say 'cheese' at any meal from breakfast to supper and between meals as well, for it is the most versatile of foods. It can be served raw or cooked and will add flavour and food value to soups, fish, meat, vegetable and egg dishes as well as making excellent desserts.

Cheese is milk which has been treated to separate the watery whey from the thick curd. It is generally made from fresh pasteurized milk. There are six steps in cheese-making and the emphasis placed upon each step by the skilled cheese-maker produces different varieties. Some cheeses ripen or mature in a few days while others may take as long as several years to develop their flavour.

Hard-pressed cheeses are the most widely known and include Cheddar, Parmesan, the holey Swiss and the smooth Dutch cheeses. They can be

Use the infinite variety of cheese to bring flavour and imagination to hot or cold dishes at any meal.

ripened for quite long periods and are often made into large cheeses. The semi-hard cheeses ripen more quickly and so have a milder flavour. Soft cheeses such as Brie and Camembert still contain some of the whey but, although they are quickly ready for eating, they soon pass the peak of their perfection. The blue-veined cheeses are lightly pressed so that the harmless, specially-introduced mould, which gives flavour and veining, is able to grow and spread. As a general rule, the hard-pressed cheeses have a longer storage life than softer ones.

Variations in flavours of cheese are caused by the pasture and water which nourish the animals from which the milk is taken. Cheese is made from the milk of cows, ewes, goats or sometimes other animals such as yaks. The milk used in the making of cheese may be whole, skimmed, sour or buttermilk, or a mixture. It may come from the evening milking, or the morning one, or a mixture of the two. Cream, thick or thin, is used alone or to enrich milk from which the cheese is made. The temperature and often the place in which the cheese is ripened are important as these determine the nature of the cheese. For example, Roquefort is ripened in caves which provide a cool, damp atmosphere.

Some cheeses do not need to be

ripened. The best examples are cottage cheese, made from whole or skimmed milk with cream or butter added; curd cheese from skimmed or buttermilk with salt added; and cream cheese from cream. Processed cheese is made by heating finely chopped cheeses together and stirring to a smooth mass which is then pasteurized. It has a bland flavour, creamy consistency and keeps for a long time.

Although most cheese is made from cows' milk, Roquefort which has been enjoyed for over 2,000 years is made from ewes' milk. Goats' milk can be made into soft or hard cheese with a mild to strong flavour. It leaves a dry, as opposed to a sweet, taste in the mouth.

The composition of cheese varies from one kind to another and so does its food value. Cheddar-type cheese is approximately one-third protein, one-third fat and one-third water. It contains calcium and vitamins A, B_2 and D. Ounce for ounce it contains more protein than meat, fish or eggs and is generally more economical. The protein is essential for building and repairing tissue and the calcium, for strong bones and teeth. Cheddar cheese contains about 120 Calories per ounce and so provides energy without bulk.

As cheese contains so much moisture, most varieties deteriorate by drying, cracking and look unappetizing. To keep cheese fresh you should wrap it tightly in a moisture-proof cling-film or transparent plastic wrap, or aluminium foil and then store it in a cool place or in the least cold part of your refrigerator. Remember to remove the cheese from the refrigerator at least half an hour before serving. It is best to buy cheese in quantities which can be consumed within a week, although correctly stored it can be kept for up to three or four weeks. When cheese becomes too dry for eating, you can grate it, wrap it well to exclude air and use it at a later date in cooking or as a garnish to soups, stews or vegetables. Cottage cheese will keep, however, for up to seven days in the refrigerator.

Cheese can be stored by deep freezing. Hard cheese tends to crumble when thawed and unripe cheese does not mature after freezing, so Camembert and similar cheese should be frozen when ripe. Grated cheese freezes well. It is convenient to weigh it into 2-ounce and 4-ounce packs so that you need only thaw the amount required at one time. In an

emergency the solid pack can be rubbed against a grater to separate without thawing.

Potted cheese is another way of preserving surplus cheese and is an excellent way of keeping blue cheeses. Cream 2 ounces [¼ cup] butter and, when soft, beat in 8 ounces cheese until smooth. To blue cheese add one to two teaspoons of brandy and a pinch of cayenne pepper. Grate hard cheese before adding to butter and add extra seasonings such as mustard, herbs and spices. Beer adds extra flavour. Eat within a day or two or cover with clarified butter and store in the refrigerator.

You will find many recipes in which cheese is either the main ingredient or a very important one. Learn to use a variety of cheese not only for your every-day meals but for special occasions. Try mixing two or more flavours such as adding a small amount of blue cheese to that served with pasta or in a salad.

Weight-watchers should eat cheese without biscuits, crackers, bread or butter. A 2-ounce portion of a semi-mild cheese with a thinly-sliced tomato makes a nutritious and slimming breakfast, a snack to be had at any time or can be eaten in place of dessert at the end of a meal.

Fruit is a natural accompaniment for cheese. Sweet, white grapes are best with blue-veined cheeses and the less sweet, black ones with the soft cheeses such as Brie. Semi-soft mild cheeses go well with ripe, well-flavoured pears.

Apple pie without cheese is said to be like a hug without a squeeze and you will find that hard cheeses give added zest to the apples in tarts and pies. For an apple pie with a difference, mix cubed cheese with the apples and bake; or just before serving, take the apple pie out of the oven, remove the pastry lid, cover the apples with thin slices of cheese, and replace the pastry lid. Heat in the oven for a few minutes until the cheese has melted. To give an apple pie a cheesy crust, put slices of cheese on an apple tart, wrap lightly in foil and heat in a hot oven for 10 minutes.

The following examples demonstrate the versatility of cheese and will give you some exciting suggestions with which to enhance your meals. Remember that cheese should never receive more heat than is necessary to melt or brown it as overcooking makes it tough and indigestible. Soft and semi-soft cheeses tend to become sticky during cooking.

Cheese bread is a tasty and nutritious base for open sandwiches. You can thicken chicken broth with eggs beaten into grated cheese, but remember not to boil the soup once the cheese has been added. You can add tiny cubes of cheese to your meatball or meat patty mixture. You will be delighted when you taste the results. Cheese mixed with chopped hard-boiled eggs makes a delicious topping for lamb chops which are baked in aluminium foil parcels.

The nutty-tasting Swiss cheeses are excellent partners for shellfish, especially shrimps or prawns. Mix the cheese and shellfish with sliced sautéed mushrooms and bake in large or small pies.

Two, three, four or more cheeses can be used in one dish. Place strips of different cheeses to decorate a salad or mix some crumbled blue cheese in the salad for an unusual flavour. Put alternate layers of cooked macaroni and several grated cheeses into a fairly deep dish; pour in a creamy sauce; top with grated Parmesan and brown.

Cottage cheese can be added with or without chives, to baked potatoes, scrambled eggs, or a bowl of soup. For a sustaining low-calorie lunch, top cottage cheese with fresh grapefruit sections and apples or other fruit in season, or mix with cooked, flaked, smoked fish to make a stuffing for tomatoes.

To make quick and easy cocktail savouries wrap strips of cheese in thinly-sliced salami and place on cocktail sticks. You can make small kebabs of cheese cubes, fruit and raw vegetables.

The usual way to make a cheese sauce is to add about 3 ounces [¾ cup] grated cheese to ½ pint [1¼ cups] white or Béchamel sauce. Cheese sauces are best served with fish, meat, egg, vegetable and pasta dishes. It is well worth trying other methods and experiment with flavours which result in original sauces.

'A good cheese deserves a good wine' is an expression which is as simple as the rule: the stronger the cheese the stronger the wine. Vintage port and ripe Stilton have long been very good partners. A full-bodied red wine is cheaper, however and suits all blue-veined cheeses. For hard and semi-hard cheeses serve a dry, fruity wine—red, rosé, or white. Soft cheeses such as Brie have a medium-strong flavour and are complemented by a fairly light red wine. Soft and creamy cheeses like a sweetish rosé or white wine. Champagne goes well with almost all cheese—so do beer and cider. The traditional English Ploughman's lunch consists of cheese, bread, butter, pickles and a glass of cider or beer.

Cheese fondue is perhaps considered by people who are unfamiliar with it as a luxury dish which is difficult to make. This is not true. The cheese fondue is simply a melted cheese dish, delicious to eat and perfect for a social occasion, especially when you are entertaining people who do not know each other very well. It is also a highlight to a wine and cheese party. The fondue pot should be placed where everybody can help himself. Each guest is given a long-handled fork on which he impales a cube of crusty bread. This is dipped into the fondue and stirred clockwise to coat the bread. Drain the cheese-dipped bread for a second or two and eat. The stirring helps to keep the fondue blended.

The versatile Cheese Fondue is easy to make and fun to serve at a party.

The Cheese Loaf decorated attractively makes an original and nutritious lunch.

Ideally the fondue is made in the kitchen in a heavy pan and then transferred to a small pot which is kept warm over a spirit burner. The pot can be refilled from the pan as required. If the mixture becomes too thick, add a little more liquid, heated first. By the time all is consumed there may well be a browned cheesy crust in the bottom of the pot. The host or hostess may decide to give this to the guest of honour as a token of regard. In Switzerland, where cheese fondue is served in cafés, it is customary for a man who lets a piece of bread drop into the fondue to buy a round of drinks. You could likewise impose an amusing penalty when you serve fondue.

The original recipe calls for Swiss wine, which is hard to find outside Switzerland, but any light dry wine will do or, as given in the recipe, cider. Instead of Swiss cheese try a local one that melts readily or a combination of two cheeses. Kirsch, the Swiss liqueur in the original recipe, is now often replaced by using a little more of the wine or cider to mix the cornflour [cornstarch] to a smooth paste.

Instead of serving bread to dip into the fondue try small pieces of cooked meat or sausage such as frankfurters, knackwurst or cabanos. Alternatively you could arrange an attractive selection of thinly-sliced chilled vegetables on a platter. Include mushrooms, carrots, cauliflower, celery, radishes, spring onions [scallions] and cucumber. Shrimps and other small shellfish may also be used to dip into the fondue. To give variation to the cheese fondue add condensed tomato purée, small pieces of cooked bacon, curry, or herbs and spices.

If you add cheese to your menus, you will find that you will have a variety of new ideas for any meal or special occasion. Do not be apprehensive of trying original ways of using cheese in your diet. Not only will your meals take on a new flavour, but you will be assured of having valuable nutrients as well.

Recipes

CIDER FONDUE
SERVES 12
1 clove garlic, cut
2 tablespoons cornflour [cornstarch]
½ teaspoon dry mustard
½ teaspoon paprika
1½ pints dry [3¾ cups hard] cider
3 lb. Cheddar cheese, or 2 lb.
  Cheddar and 1 lb. sharp cheese,
  grated

Rub the inside of a heavy saucepan with the garlic. Blend cornflour [cornstarch], mustard and paprika with 4 tablespoons of cider. Put remaining cider into the pan and warm over a gentle heat. Add the cheese and stir until melted. Then stir in

the cornflour [cornstarch] mixture. Bring to the boil and simmer gently until creamy, stirring constantly. Serve as previously described.

PUFFED CHEESE AND HAM SLICES
MAKES 20—24 SLICES
7½ oz. frozen puff pastry, thawed
1 egg
4 oz. [1 cup] cheese, grated
  prepared mustard, salt and pepper
4 oz. [½ cup] cooked ham, chopped
1 teaspoon chutney

Preheat the oven to 425°F, Gas Mark 7, 220°C.

Roll the pastry into a very thin oblong and cut in half. Mix egg, cheese and seasonings and spread over one half of the pastry, right to the edges. Mix ham with chutney and scatter on top. Cover with the other half of the pastry and press well together. Brush the top with milk, cut into 20 to 24 'fingers' with a very sharp knife and place on greased baking trays. Bake for about 15 minutes.

CHEESE AND TOMATO PUDDING
SERVES 4
5 oz. [1¼ cups] sharp cheese, grated
4 oz. [2 cups] fresh breadcrumbs
  mustard, salt and cayenne pepper
2 eggs, separated
½ pint [1¼ cups] milk
8 small tomatoes
  grated Parmesan

Mix together the cheese, breadcrumbs and seasonings. In another bowl, mix the egg yolks together. Warm the milk and pour it over the eggs. Beat well and pour over the dry ingredients. Leave for about 10 minutes.

Preheat the oven to 350°F, Gas Mark 4, 180°C. Whisk the egg whites until very stiff and fold them into the mixture.

Grease an ovenproof dish. Slice the tomatoes and arrange some around the sides of the dish. Pour in the cheese mixture, without disturbing the tomatoes. Top with the rest of the tomatoes and sprinkle with Parmesan. Bake for 35 minutes or until the pudding is set and lightly browned.

CHEESE AND ONION ROLLS
MAKES 18 SMALL ROLLS
  shortcrust pastry using 6 oz.
  [1½ cups] flour
1 medium-sized onion, chopped
1 small apple, chopped
3 oz. [¾ cup] cheese, grated
1 oz. [½ cup] fresh breadcrumbs
  mustard, salt and pepper
1 egg, beaten

Preheat the oven to 400°F, Gas Mark 6, 200°C.

Roll the pastry into a long strip 8 inches wide. Cut in half to get 2 strips 4 inches wide.

Mix the onion, apple, cheese, breadcrumbs and seasonings with most of the beaten egg. Put this mixture along each

46

pastry strip near one edge and brush the other edge with a little beaten egg. Roll the pastry over the filling until the second edge is underneath. Brush with beaten egg and make diagonal slits all along the top of the pastry. Cut each pastry roll into 9 portions and place them on a greased baking tray. Bake for 20 to 25 minutes.

CHEESE LOAF
SERVES 8

12 oz. [3 cups] **cheese, grated**
 4 oz. [1 cup] **walnuts, chopped**
 mustard, salt and cayenne pepper
 8 oz. [1 cup] **cottage cheese**
 4 oz. [½ cup] **mayonnaise**
 ½ oz. **gelatin dissolved in 3**
 tablespoons hot water

Mix the cheese, walnuts and seasonings together and fold in the cottage cheese and mayonnaise with the dissolved gelatin. Pour into a greased loaf tin and turn out on to a serving dish when set. Decorate attractively.

SIMPLE CHEESE SAUCE
 1 small can **evaporated milk**
 4 oz. [1 cup] **cheese, grated**
 mustard, salt and cayenne pepper

Put all the ingredients into a saucepan. Heat and stir gently, but do not boil, until the cheese melts.

TWO-FLAVOUR CHEESE SAUCE
 1 can **condensed cream**
 soup—mushroom, chicken
 ½ **soup can milk**
 4 oz. [1 cup] **cheese, grated**

Mix all the ingredients together in a saucepan. Stir and heat, but do not boil, until the cheese melts to make a smooth sauce.

STRAWBERRY CHEESECAKE
SERVES 8—10

 6 oz. [2 cups] **digestive biscuit**
 [graham cracker] crumbs
1½ oz. [⅓ cup] **light brown sugar**
 6 tablespoons **butter, melted**
 2 **eggs, separated**
 3 oz. **castor [6 tablespoons fine] sugar**
 8 oz. **strawberries**
 ½ oz. **gelatin**
12 oz. [1½ cups] **cottage cheese, sieved**
 ¾ pint double [1⅞ cups heavy] **cream, whipped**

Mix together the crumbs, sugar and butter in a bowl. Put into a greased 8-inch pie plate or loose-bottomed shallow cake tin and press evenly over the base and sides. Chill.

Whisk the egg yolks and the sugar in a basin over hot, not boiling, water until the yolks are cooked and the mixture is thick. Leave to cool, whisking occasionally.

Rub the strawberries through a nylon sieve to obtain a purée.

Dissolve the gelatin in 3 tablespoons of hot water, stirring with a bright metal spoon which will show any undissolved particles. Add the gelatin to the egg yolk mixture with the strawberry purée, sieved cottage cheese and half the cream.

Whisk the egg whites until very stiff and fold into the mixture. Spoon this mixture into the crumb-lined tin and smooth the top. When set, decorate with the remaining cream and the extra strawberries cut in halves.

COTTAGE CREAM
SERVES 4

 4 oz. **cream cheese**
 8 oz. [1 cup] **cottage cheese, sieved**
 grated rind and juice of 1 orange
 or lemon
 4 teaspoons **sugar**
 1 **egg white**

In a bowl, beat the cream cheese until it becomes soft. Beat in the sieved cottage cheese, fruit rind and juice and sugar.

In another bowl, whisk the egg white until it is very stiff and fold it into the cheese mixture.

Divide between 4 small glasses and chill before serving or put alternate layers of fruit and cream in tall glasses.

Salad Days

There are many exciting ways and reasons for serving a salad. In France, a fresh green salad tossed in a simple vinaigrette follows the main course to aid the digestion and to refresh the palate before the next course is served. In the United States a side bowl of salad serves as an accompaniment throughout the meal. A salad can also make a substantial and nutritious main course for lunch or dinner. While salads are generally low in calories, they contain important vitamins and mineral salts. In most weight-reducing diets, for these reasons, fresh green salads do not feature in the restricted food list. It is the mayonnaise and oil dressings high in calories that need to be avoided. Tasty, low-calorie dressings, however, can be made from tomato juice or unsweetened fruit juices.

Depending on the seasonal ingredients available and your personal taste, salads can be as plain or as elaborate as you choose to make them. If a salad is to act as a main dish, it should include some protein, such as meat, fish, eggs or cheese. When a salad is to be served as an hors-d'oeuvre or appetizer it could be made up of crudités. These are raw, usually crisp, vegetables such as cucumber, radishes, celery, sweet peppers, tomatoes and mushrooms thinly sliced or cut in fingers, or as for carrots, very finely grated. The crudités are served with a dressing of oil and lemon juice. Sometimes tuna fish or a slice of salami or ham is added. As a side dish with a main meal, a plain green salad tossed in French dressing is an ideal accompaniment to a grilled or broiled dish or, you could serve an orange salad with roast duck. When, however, the main course is very richly flavoured, a crisp green salad can be served after the main course to refresh the palate. Salads can be used as fillings for sandwiches or rolls or for a Scandinavian open sandwich which is a meal in itself. A variety of complementing and blending salads can be presented with cold meats, poultry, fish or game to make an attractive cold table or buffet.

Use delicate salad vegetables with their wonderful range of contrasting and harmonizing colours from the pale bitter green of a succulent young lettuce, through the soft greens of cucumber and cauliflower to the glowing reds of tomatoes to give full play to your creative cooking talents. To preserve their freshness, salad vegetables need to be handled with care from the time they are very young plants until they are fully matured. Unless you grow your own vegetables you can only control the quality of the vegetables when you buy them, so choose your vegetables with care and make sure you never buy coarse or wilting produce. Choose crisp, brightly-coloured, unblemished salad vegetables. Small, young, tender produce is sweet and full of nutrients; overgrown salad vegetables tend to be coarse, tough, flavourless and will have lost some of the nutrients.

Salad greens, such as lettuce, need washing and careful drying by shaking and then pressing them gently on an absorbent towel or kitchen paper. If you are not going to use the greens immediately put them in a cool place or in the salad compartment of a refrigerator.

There is an infinite variety of salad greens to choose from and they each have their own particular characteristics which give different taste appeal and texture to salads.

Belgian Endive—the long, smooth

Salads can be eaten throughout the year. They are nutritious, refreshing and generally low in calories.

leaves are a pale cream with a golden tip, very crisp and slightly peppery in flavour. Use this plant with lettuce or plain with a vinaigrette dressing.

Curly Endive or Chicory—this is a curly, pale green plant with a bitterish tang. It can be used instead of lettuce and blends well with grapefruit and orange segments.

Escarole—this looks rather like a tightly crimped lettuce. The leaves are dark green, edged with yellow. The taste resembles Belgian Endive but is blander.

Lambs' Tongues or Field Lettuce—this is also known as corn salad. It is dark green with elongated leaves rather like spinach. Use in a mixed green salad.

Spinach—the young tender leaves add an unusual flavour to a green salad.

Dandelion leaves—use the young shoots which have a sharp, fresh taste to give a tang to a green salad.

Watercress—this is a dark green, leafy plant with a peppery flavour. A bed of watercress could be covered with slices of red tomatoes and a simple dressing.

Lettuces—there are many varieties ranging from the round, firm cabbage lettuce, to the cos [Romaine] with its long spoon-shaped leaves.

Nasturtium leaves—these give tang to salads when used discreetly.

When you are preparing a salad choose ingredients and garnishes which will

complement in colour, flavour and texture the dish it is to accompany. Here are some ideas for making salads which can be created from one or two vegetables and/or fruits. Add a piquant garnish and a dressing or sauce which will enhance hot or cold fish, meat and poultry dishes as well as making attractive starters.

Thinly slice firm, ripe tomatoes, garnish with a few chopped celery leaves or fresh mint and lightly dress with a French dressing seasoned with a crushed clove of garlic. This type of salad is a favourite in Mediterranean countries when it is garnished with black olives and served with a chunk of fresh brown bread to absorb the delicious dressing.

Slice unpeeled cucumber and dress it with plain yogurt lightly beaten and seasoned with the faint anis flavour of dill weed. Sour cream sharpened with lemon juice can replace the yogurt.

Button or cup mushrooms can be sliced paper thin, garnished with chopped parsley or chives and tossed in a French dressing spiced with a tablespoon of tomato ketchup.

Finely shredded red cabbage, a coarsely grated apple and a few chopped dates can be flavoured with caraway seeds and dressed with a tangy French dressing into which 1 or 2 tablespoons of plain yogurt have been beaten.

A medley of lightly cooked green beans, broad beans or lima beans, and French beans can be tossed in mayonnaise and garnished with toasted almonds.

Chop fresh celery, chicory and unpeeled red apple and dress with mayonnaise, spiked with capers or chopped gherkins.

Cook leeks until just tender, slice them and top with a cream cheese dressing and garnish with parsley, or walnuts.

Serve bean sprouts and slivers of stem ginger with a peppery French dressing.

Moisten segments of grapefruit and orange garnished with almonds or walnuts with a vinaigrette sauce.

Small florets of crunchy fresh cauliflower can be added to a plain green salad to give variation in texture and a slightly spicy flavour. Serve with cream or mayonnaise dressing, lightened with the grated peel and juice of an orange.

An imaginative dressing creates a subtle balance of flavours which can transform the simplest salad into a perfect dish. A salad dressing should enhance salad vegetables and not overwhelm them. A vinaigrette or French dressing is the ideal accompaniment for a delicate green salad, while home-made mayonnaise or salad creams with a tangy garnish give body and additional food value to a main course salad.

The simplest dressing is a French dressing made up of 3 parts salad oil to 1 part wine vinegar or lemon juice, seasoned with French mustard, a pinch of sugar to taste and salt and pepper. A French dressing can be changed into a sophisticated vinaigrette sauce with the addition of finely chopped herbs such as

chives, chervil, tarragon, dill weed, parsley, sweet basil or marjoram which are chosen to complement the salad vegetable used, such as sweet basil with tomatoes. For convenience you can make up a quantity of French dressing, bottle it and store it in a cool place. It will keep for about a week.

Home-made mayonnaise is a combination of egg yolks, seasoning and olive oil added drop by drop until the mayonnaise is thick and smooth. Lemon juice

or wine vinegar is added to sharpen the flavour. A quick and delicious mayonnaise can be quickly made by whisking French dressing into cream with a little prepared mustard and sugar to taste. There are, however, a number of excellent egg-based salad creams and mayonnaises on the market, which can be given your own individual flavouring.

Sliced cherries in the mayonnaise complement a ham salad. Chopped orange segments and a little grated orange rind

are delicious with veal or pork salads. Add a small quantity of tomato purée, curry powder or chopped herbs to a salad cream and serve with chicken or fish salads. Beat some fresh or sour cream into a mayonnaise, lighten with strained apple juice and serve with any cold spicy meat. A suitable cocktail salad cream for shrimps, prawns or tuna fish is to blend 1 tablespoon of mild mustard, $\frac{1}{4}$ teaspoon of grated onion, 1 tablespoon of chopped olives with $\frac{1}{4}$ pint [5 fluid ounces] of mayonnaise and $\frac{1}{4}$ pint [5 fluid ounces] of cream.

Winter, summer, spring or fall you can make salads for any occasion. With such a seasonal variety of salad vegetables, an assortment of dressings and imagination it will be easy to make salads interesting in presentation and taste. Do not be afraid to use unusual and original combinations when combining your salad ingredients. Salad days are every day, throughout the year.

Recipes

RUSSIAN SPRING SALAD
SERVES 4—6
  4 oz. young carrots
  4 oz. new potatoes
  4 oz. green beans, fresh or frozen
  4 oz. peas, fresh or frozen
      cauliflower florets
  6-8 tablespoons French dressing
  1 tablespoon capers
  2-3 hard-boiled eggs, shelled and
      quartered
  1 tablespoon chopped parsley

Prepare the vegetables; dice the carrots and potatoes. Cook the vegetables in boiling salted water until just tender but still crisp. Drain well.

Stir the capers into the French dressing. While the vegetables are still warm toss them lightly in the dressing until well coated.

Pile the dressed vegetables on to a shallow dish and arrange the egg quarters around the salad. Garnish with chopped parsley. Serve with meat, fish, poultry or cheese dishes. To make a more substantial salad suitable for a main meal, cooked meat or poultry can be added.

FRENCH GREEN SALAD
SERVES 4
  1 round [Boston] lettuce
  1 teaspoon chopped fresh mint
      French dressing
  1 medium-sized cooked beetroot
      [beet], finely sliced
  2 hard-boiled eggs, shelled and
      quartered

Place the lettuce leaves, in the shape of a lettuce, in the centre of a dish. Garnish with mint and lightly dress with French dressing. Arrange a ring of sliced beetroot [beet] around the lettuce and decorate with the quartered hard-boiled eggs.

MACARONI AND SALAMI SALAD
SERVES 4—6
  8-12 slices salami
  1 Spanish [Bermuda] onion, peeled
      and thinly sliced
  1 red or green pepper, deseeded
      and thinly sliced
  4 oz. button mushrooms, sliced
  2 tablespoons chopped parsley
  8 oz. macaroni, cooked and well
      drained
  6-8 tablespoons French dressing
  1 clove garlic, crushed

Cut the salami into strips and combine with the onion, sweet pepper, mushrooms, parsley and macaroni. Toss lightly.

Combine the French dressing and crushed garlic, beat well and pour over the salad. Mix lightly and serve.

A salad which uses pasta is best served as a separate course. The pasta must be well drained and cool before it is mixed with other ingredients.

SALAD WALDORF
SERVES 4
  2 red eating apples, cored and diced
  2 green eating apples, cored and diced
    lemon juice
  2 tablespoons chopped walnuts
  1 medium-sized celeriac, cut into thin strips
    French dressing
    watercress for garnish

Toss the apples, unpeeled, in lemon juice to prevent them from turning brown. Add the walnuts, leaving a few for garnish, and the celeriac. Coat the ingredients with the French dressing and mix well.

Turn into an attractive salad dish. Decorate with the remaining walnuts, and arrange the watercress around the edge of the dish. Serve this crisp salad with grills or as a side dish.

SWEET AND SOUR RICE
SERVES 4
  8 oz. [1¼ cups] long-grain rice, cooked and well drained
  ½ green or red pepper, deseeded and finely sliced
  3 bananas, peeled and sliced
  1 tablespoon chives or shallots, finely chopped
  1 tablespoon chopped toasted almonds
    watercress for garnish
Cream dressing:
  1 tablespoon salad oil
  1 tablespoon wine vinegar
  1 teaspoon sugar
  2 tablespoons sour cream
  1 teaspoon tomato purée
Mix together in a salad bowl the rice, sweet pepper, bananas, chives or shallots and almonds.

Combine the cream dressing ingredients and whisk well. Pour the dressing over the salad mixture and toss lightly until well mixed. Garnish with watercress. Serve this salad with cold meat or cheese.

SALADE MARGUERITE
SERVES 4
  4 sweet seedless oranges
  1 grapefruit
 16 grapes, halved and pipped
6-8 tablespoons French dressing
  1 small lettuce
    chopped walnuts for garnish

Remove the rind and pith from the oranges and the grapefruit. Divide the oranges into segments and dice the grapefruit. Mix all the fruit together. Pour the French dressing over the fruit and mix lightly.

Place the lettuce leaves on the bottom of a shallow dish, arrange the fruit mixture on top and garnish with chopped walnuts. Serve this savoury fruit salad with a rich game dish such as braised duck or pigeon.

PIQUANT TOMATO MOULD WITH SPICED CHICKEN
SERVES 4—6
  4 teaspoons gelatin
  1 pint [2½ cups] tomato juice
  1 teaspoon sugar
  1 teaspoon tomato ketchup
  1 tablespoon lemon juice
  2 tablespoons finely chopped chives or shallots
    Worcestershire sauce
Spiced chicken filling:
  5 fl. oz. plain yogurt
  2 tablespoons French dressing
  ½ teaspoon curry powder
  8 oz. cooked chicken, diced

Dissolve the gelatin in 4 tablespoons of hot tomato juice. Mix together the remaining tomato juice, sugar, tomato ketchup, lemon juice, chives or shallots and a dash of Worcestershire sauce. Stir the dissolved gelatin into the tomato liquid. Pour this mixture into a lightly oiled or wetted ring mould. Set aside in a cool place or place in a refrigerator for two to three hours or until the mixture is set.

Lightly whip the yogurt until it is creamy. Add the French dressing and curry powder and beat until they are well blended with the yogurt. Mix the chicken into the yogurt dressing.

Turn out the tomato mould carefully onto a round dish and fill the centre with the spicy chicken mixture. Spoon the rest of the mixture around the base of the mould. Serve with a crisp, green, side salad.

As a variation, any chopped cold meat, poultry or fish mixed with the yogurt dressing can be used as a filling for the tomato mould.

SPICY PINEAPPLE CREAM SALAD
SERVES 4—6
  8 oz. cream cheese
  3 teaspoons prepared mustard
  5 fl. oz. plain yogurt, lightly beaten until creamy
    salt and pepper
  8 oz. canned crushed pineapple, drained
  7 oz. canned pork luncheon meat, diced
  2 tablespoons chopped walnuts

Beat together the cream cheese and mustard until well mixed. Stir in the yogurt and season to taste.

Mix in the pineapple, luncheon meat and chopped nuts, reserving a few nuts for garnish.

Pile the salad on to an attractive dish and chill. Garnish with the remaining chopped nuts and serve with a plain green salad.

These are three variations: use chopped mandarin oranges instead of pineapple; stir in 2 tablespoons sultanas or raisins with the dry ingredients; for a lighter salad, omit the luncheon meat.

CREOLE SALAD WITH SHRIMPS
SERVES 4
  1 lb. potatoes
  2 tablespoons chopped chives or shallots
  4 oz. prawns or shrimps, peeled
  5 fl. oz. mayonnaise
  1 tablespoon tomato ketchup
  ½ red or green pepper, finely sliced, for garnish

Wash the potatoes and boil them in their skins. When cooked, drain and remove the skins. Dice the potatoes and, while they are still warm, blend them with the chives or shallots, prawns, mayonnaise and tomato ketchup. Allow the salad to cool and then garnish with sliced pepper and serve.

As variations, omit the prawns and add finely diced Cheddar cheese or garnish with freshly chopped mint instead of the sweet pepper.

CREAM CHEESE DRESSING
SERVES 4
  8 oz. cream cheese
  2 tablespoons lemon juice
  4 tablespoons salad oil
    salt and pepper
  1 teaspoon chopped fresh mint

Mix together the cream cheese and lemon juice. Beat in the oil gradually until you have a smooth consistency. Season to taste with salt and pepper. Gently mix in the mint.

Other variations of this Cream Cheese Dressing can be made by using chopped chives or parsley instead of the mint; adding some chopped nuts; adding a clove of garlic, crushed, with the cream cheese and lemon juice; or using garlic salt in place of plain salt.

CURRY DRESSING
MAKES 5 FLUID OUNCES
  2 teaspoons brown sugar
  ½ teaspoon salt
    pepper
  1 teaspoon curry powder
  4 tablespoons lemon juice
  6 tablespoons salad oil

Combine all the ingredients and beat very well together until blended. This piquant dressing is delicious with poultry, rice and pasta dishes.

LOW-CALORIE DRESSING
2 SERVINGS
  2 tablespoons lemon juice
  2 tablespoons fresh orange juice
  ½ teaspoon prepared mustard
    salt and pepper to taste
  2 teaspoons chopped parsley, chives or dill weed

Whisk all the ingredients together until well blended. As a variation you could omit the lemon and orange juice and use 4 tablespoons of tomato juice.

Cook for Health

"A man seldom thinks of anything with more earnestness than he does of his dinner," said Dr. Samuel Johnson in the eighteenth century. And even today many of us think, sometimes obsessively, about what we eat, about dieting to lose weight, about economizing on the food we buy and about pleasing our families and friends with the food we serve them.

But all too often such thoughts tend to obscure the equally important part food plays in keeping us healthy. For good health is basically derived from eating good food, which is carefully prepared and well cooked.

Any food you buy has a certain nutritional value. It is then up to you to see that the food is treated in ways that will preserve the maximum amount of this potential nutritional value. Food should always be treated with respect. With wise and careful buying you can ensure that you get the most nutrients for your money. If you start with a high concentration of nutrients in the raw food, you stand the best chance of getting an adequate supply of nutrients to the table. To do this successfully you should know how to handle each type of food and to take the simple precautions necessary to minimize nutrient loss.

Don't be like Sally who can't resist a bargain. Her local supermarket was offering some pale and limp cabbages (loss of vitamins A and C), at well below regular prices. Sally bought two pounds for her family's evening meal. She chopped the cabbage up and soaked it in cold water for 30 minutes (loss of vitamin C), "just to make absolutely sure it's clean and to freshen it up," while she prepared the rest of the meal. She then boiled the cabbage in a large quantity of water for 15 minutes and squeezed it to drain away the water (complete loss of any remaining vitamin C). She served her family the result—three-quarters of a pound of roughage with virtually no other nutritive value.

Fruit and vegetables are, in fact, particularly susceptible to deterioration in quality and nutrient value. They are the major sources of vitamin C in our diets and vitamin C is the most unstable of all vitamins. It is destroyed by combination with oxygen in the air, and the heat of cooking will speed up this reaction. Vitamin C is also soluble in water and can be easily soaked or washed out of fruit or vegetables. So it is a good idea to train yourself to react to fruit and vegetables as if each piece carries a

"highly perishable" or "fragile" label and treat it accordingly.

When you are buying fruit and vegetables it makes a good nutritional sense to check that they have no blemishes or bruises. Examine them closely in the shop to reassure yourself that they are quite fresh and sound. Never be persuaded to buy, as Sally was, wilted, shrivelled or aged fruit or vegetables. The vitamin C content of fresh fruit and vegetables falls off quite rapidly with time. So don't buy large quantities of fresh fruit or vegetables if you are not sure you will be able to use them in two or three days.

Ideally, you should buy fruit and vegetables on the day you are going to cook and eat them. But this is not always convenient or practical. If you do have to store the fruit and vegetables you have bought, be sure that each piece is quite dry, otherwise it will soon start to rot. Wrap green, leafy vegetables, such as spinach and cabbage, loosely in paper if they are to be stored in a cool, dark kitchen cupboard or put them in the refrigerator in a covered plastic box. Do not allow too much air to circulate about them because this promotes wilting and loss of vitamin C. Leafy vegetables kept

at room temperature can lose as much as half of their vitamins B and C in one day. But never allow leafy vegetables to freeze in the refrigerator. Slow freezing allows large ice crystals to form which damages the cells.

Keep root vegetables in plastic bags. Make small holes in the bags for ventilation or the vegetables will rot. Do not store them for more than four days. They soon shrivel and lose their nutrient value. If you buy fruit which is not quite ripe, let it ripen at room temperature for a couple of days and then put it in the refrigerator.

The key to properly preparing and cooking fruit and vegetables is speed. Because of the instability of vitamin C it is best to organize yourself so that the preparation-cooking-serving sequence takes as little time as possible.

When you prepare green leafy vegetables, do not cut away too many of the darker green outer leaves because these contain the greatest concentration of vitamins and minerals. Just take extra care to wash them thoroughly. Only use cold water for washing vegetables. And since vitamin C is so soluble in water, under no circumstances should vegetables be soaked to freshen them. If you feel that vegetables need freshening put them in the refrigerator.

As a general rule, restrict your handling of vegetables to a bare minimum. The skins on such foods as apples and oranges or potatoes protect the flesh from contact with oxygen, so it is only when vegetables and fruit are cut, chopped, peeled, grated or sliced that a large surface area is exposed to the air and light—two of the great enemies of vitamin C. When cutting food always use a sharp knife which will slice cleanly through the flesh rather than a blunt one that tears and damages the tissues. You can prevent such sliced fruits as bananas or apples from discolouring by sprinkling lemon juice over them, and because vitamin C is more stable in acid condi-

Formula 1 for nutrient loss—boil vegetables in a large amount of water in an open pan for a long time.

tions, this also protects the fruit from vitamin loss.

Make it a rule to peel vegetables only when the skin is very tough, bitter or too uneven to be cleaned thoroughly. Well-scrubbed carrots, sliced and cooked for just a few minutes in a covered pan with one ounce of butter and just one tablespoon of water, taste far sweeter than those that are peeled. Try boiling potatoes in their skins, too. Then, if you want to, you can easily peel the skins away after they are cooked. And such vegetables as carrots and parsnips, as well as potatoes, can be baked dry in their skins and served with melted butter.

Because some vitamins are gradually destroyed when they are exposed to light and air, only prepare your vegetables as you require them and then plunge them straight into a little fast-boiling water. Let the water boil for a couple of minutes before adding the vegetables. This helps to drive off any oxygen dissolved in the water which would otherwise react with and inactivate the vitamin C that the vegetables contain.

Most people automatically salt vegetables at the beginning of cooking. This is an infallible way to draw all the delicious juices and flavours out of the vegetables. So it is better, except when you are cooking vegetables in a sauce, to salt them lightly just before serving. You can add butter and freshly-ground pepper at this stage, too.

Boiling water is, in fact, the worst form of soaking since it compounds the evils of heat and water. Some of the water-soluble vitamins B and C will dissolve into the cooking water. To avoid excessive losses, always cook vegetables for the shortest possible time in the smallest amount of water. Lightly-cooked vegetables not only taste nicer, they are also much better for you. Always cook vegetables in a covered pan to maintain an even temperature throughout the pan and to exclude light and air. Never add bicarbonate of soda to the water when

you are cooking vegetables because this destroys vitamin C.

Of course, there are many better ways of cooking vegetables other than boiling them in a pan of water and discarding most of the health-giving vitamins and minerals with the cooking liquid. Because all fresh vegetables contain a large amount of water, they can be cooked in a covered pan, with a tight-fitting lid so that no steam escapes, with no added water at all. If you like, add a little butter and keep shaking the pan so that the vegetables won't stick to the bottom of the pan and burn. This method works very well for carrots and such green leafy vegetables as spinach and cabbage.

For a change you can also try simmering vegetables in a little milk instead of in water. Vegetables cooked this way taste milder and sweeter than those simmered in water. And you can then use the milk to make a sauce. It also makes a delicious drink.

One great asset for any nutrient-conscious cook is a steamer. In a steamer the vegetables are placed in the pan on a perforated platform above the water level in the steam rising from the boiling water. Because the vegetables do not actually sit in the water, nutrients cannot dissolve out. Potatoes, carrots, French beans and cauliflower are particularly good when they are cooked in this way.

No matter which method you choose to cook your vegetables, try to resist the temptation to mash or purée them when they are cooked. This may add to the appeal of the vegetables and increase the variety of ways in which you can serve them, but it will also destroy much of the remaining vitamins.

Always serve vegetables as soon as they are cooked. Keeping food hot only tends to further reduce its nutrient content. It may require more time and effort, but it makes good nutritional sense to cook vegetables only as they are required. Storing cooked food in the refrigerator for 24 hours can result in a 25 per cent loss of remaining vitamin C. Reheating causes still greater losses.

This deterioration in nutrient value which is a result of cooking is most marked when fruit and vegetables could be eaten raw rather than cooked. Some raw vegetables and at least one piece of fresh fruit should be eaten each day. A green salad, tossed in a piquant vinaigrette or lemon and oil dressing, makes an appetizing start to any meal or even a light meal in its own right with the addition of some good protein source such as cheese or egg. And the acid content of salad dressings helps to ensure that the vitamin C is unspoiled.

Although much emphasis has been placed upon the vulnerability of fruit and vegetables to nutrient losses, the same principles of care, thought, planning and timing hold good for the selection and cooking of meat as well. Don't be tempted to buy totally lean meat. Instead choose meat which is marbled with fat, because a little fat is essential in cooking, so that the meat retains more of its natural flavours and juices.

Always unpack meat from the butcher's paper or plastic packaging and store it in the refrigerator, covered but with plenty of room for air to circulate around it. Bacteria multiply more rapidly in an airless atmosphere and decomposition sets in more quickly as a result. But never keep meat, even in the refrigerator, for more than three days.

The secret of cooking meat lies in reaching a formula which combines ways of retaining maximum flavour and nutrients with cooking for tenderness. Meat is a muscle tissue and high temperatures tend to toughen the protein fibres of this muscle. In raw meats these fibres are soft, delicate and malleable. When cooked slowly at low temperatures such fibres merely become firm.

Roasting temperatures can destroy as much as one half of the heat-destructible vitamin B_1 (thiamine) of the meat. Grilling, or broiling, causes a loss of about one-third of vitamin B_2. So it is important, when you have grilled or roasted meat, to use the pan juices which contain at least some of these lost nutrients, to make a sauce or a gravy. If you are cooking meat in a casserole, quickly fry the meat first to seal in the

Become a nutrient-conscious cook. Stop wasting vitamins by washing, cutting or cooking them away in the kitchen.

nutrients. The problem of capturing the nutrients does not arise with stews since the juices are incorporated and eaten in the sauce anyway.

Some losses from cooking meat can be beneficial, especially if you are on a weight-reducing or low-fat diet. For fat is as much a nutrient as any vitamin, but is not necessarily in such limited supply or as desirable. It is possible to promote greater loss of fat by using a grill, or broiler, which allows the fat to drip away.

But to prevent loss of valuable juices during grilling, broiling or frying, brush the meat thoroughly with oil. Moisture cannot escape through a layer of oil. As with vegetables, it is not desirable to sprinkle the surface of the meat with salt before cooking because this tends to draw out the juices.

Fish is another, and all too often neglected, source of protein. But fish is a highly perishable food and should be cooked and eaten within 24 hours of being bought.

Everybody knows that milk turns sour if it is kept for a long time. But few people give very much thought to the nutrient losses that can result from careless treatment of milk. If milk is exposed to light for a long time its vitamin B_2 (riboflavin) content is greatly diminished, so do not leave milk bottles standing on the doorstep in the sunlight for any length of time. If you cannot be there to take it indoors, provide some shading or cover to protect the milk from the light. Tinted milk bottles and opaque cartons also help to protect the milk from the destructive effects of light. Always keep milk in the refrigerator in a bottle with the cap on. Do not pour milk into the bottle from a jug.

As far as such dry cereal products as bread, cakes, biscuits or pasta are concerned, the aim is to keep them as fresh as possible and at the same time preserve the maximum quantity of nutrients. Store bread in a dark, ventilated bin. Bread is a source of vitamins of the B group and some of these are light sensitive. The same is true of pasta. Macaroni and spaghetti may look attractive in a bottle on the kitchen shelf but they do suffer significant losses of light-sensitive nutrients kept that way.

Many people wonder whether different cooking principles and methods have to be applied to "convenience" foods of the frozen, canned and dried varieties. The arguments for convenience foods in terms of ease of preparation and availability out of season, and against, in terms of loss of flavour and expense, are numerous but the only relevant argument really relates to nutrient losses.

In the case of canned foods, processing has already reduced their nutrient content. So, instead of heating the contents of the tin again which only causes a further loss of nutrients, try using vegetables straight from the tin in salads. Asparagus, beans and peas are all good served in this way. And this avoids heating the contents of the tin again and causing further loss of nutrients.

Frozen vegetables do not suffer from quite the same degree of loss. The sheer speed and efficiency of modern freezing techniques means that frozen green beans, for example, will quite possibly provide you with more nutrients than the soft and floppy green beans which are frequently all you can buy from the supermarket. But never cut a packet of frozen vegetables open and leave them to thaw out in the kitchen. This exposes the vegetables quite unnecessarily to air and light. Most manufacturers suggest tipping the vegetables straight from the freezer into boiling water.

Always follow the cooking instructions on the packet or can quite meticulously. They have been designed specifically for that product so that you get the most flavour and nutrients.

Getting the most out of your food in terms of nutrients and flavour, and hence health and enjoyment, may take a little more thought and planning. But if you want to be sure that the food you finally serve your family or friends contains sufficient nutrients to meet the requirements of their bodies these simple precautions and rules are well worth the effort. Indeed in many cases it is easier to cook this way than by over-washing, over-cutting and over-cooking.

Keep the Goodness in Your Food

Food	Storage	Best preparation	Source of
Apples Keep in a cool room		Peel only when necessary. Rub cut apples with lemon juice so that they will not turn brown. When stewing, use only a tiny bit of water	Very little vitamin C
Artichokes, globe 2 to 3 days in a dark, dry place or covered in the refrigerator		Wash under running water. Trim the stems, remove tough outer leaves and cut off the spiky tips of inner leaves. Rub cut places with lemon juice to prevent discolouration. Cook in boiling, salted water for 20 to 30 minutes. Serve hot with melted butter or cold with vinaigrette sauce	A little of vitamins B_1 and C
Asparagus 2 days in a plastic bag in the refrigerator		Wash carefully. Cut off a little of thick white base of stalks. Tie in bunches and steam for about 25 minutes. Serve with melted butter	Vitamin C
Aubergine [Eggplant] 3 days in warmest part of refrigerator or crisper drawer		Wash. Remove any hard stalk. Bake in casserole with butter and a little milk for 30 minutes	Vitamin B group. Very little vitamin C
Bananas Keep in a cool place—never in the refrigerator		Eat raw, in salads (particularly good with coconut) or fried as a dessert or accompaniment to pork or chicken	Very little vitamin C
Beans, green Buy only on the day they are needed or they will go limp		Wash and string. Leave French beans whole. Thinly slice runner beans. Cook quickly in a very little boiling water until barely tender. Drain, salt and toss in melted butter	Vitamin C and a little iron
Beetroot [Beets] Up to a week, loosely wrapped in a cool, dark place		Wash and boil until tender when pierced with a fork. Peel and serve hot with hollandaise sauce. To serve cold with salads, allow to cool unpeeled until required	A little iron
Blackcurrants Buy only on the day they are needed		Eat fresh with a little sugar and cream, or mash and stew with brown sugar until just tender	Very rich in vitamin C
Broccoli Buy only on day needed to prevent withering		Wash quickly in cold, running water. Steam until just tender and serve with melted butter or hollandaise sauce	Vitamin C and iron

Food	Storage	Best preparation	Source of
Brussels sprouts 2 to 3 days in a plastic bag in the refrigerator		Wash quickly and trim, but leave whole. Cook quickly in boiling water until just tender. Salt and serve with butter and freshly ground black pepper	Vitamin C and iron
Cabbage 3 to 4 days in a plastic bag in the refrigerator		Wash, Shred finely with a very sharp knife. Bring to the boil in milk. Drain. Make a white sauce with milk and pour over the cabbage in a fireproof dish. Dot with breadcrumbs and a little butter. Bake in moderate oven for 20 minutes. Best of all served raw, finely shredded, in salads	Vitamin C and iron
Carrots 2 to 3 days in a cool, dark place		Wash thoroughly, but do not peel or scrape. Melt 1 tablespoon of butter in 1 tablespoon of water in a pan. Toss carrots in this and partly cover. Cook for about 10 minutes over a low heat, shaking occasionally. Salt, sprinkle with freshly-chopped parsley and serve	Vitamin A, a little vitamin C
Cauliflower 2 days in refrigerator, or 1 day loosely wrapped in paper in a cool, dark place		Wash quickly under cold, running water. Divide head into small florets and steam for 10 to 15 minutes. Serve with cheese or sauce made with freshly-chopped parsley	A little vitamin C, and some iron
Celery 2 to 3 days in refrigerator if possible		Eat raw, after washing, in salads and with cheese. Or braise in a covered dish in a moderate oven	Very little vitamin C
Cheese About 1 week, covered, in a cool, dark place		Use fresh or in any favourite recipes, but never cook for any length of time	Protein and vitamin A. High in calcium
Chicken Fresh—only keep 1 day in refrigerator. Frozen—cook immediately after defrosting		Use any recipe you choose, but try to use the juices from the bird in a sauce or gravy	Protein. A little of the B-group vitamins
Courgettes [Zucchini] 2 days in refrigerator		Wash, cut off stem end and slice thinly without peeling. Toss in melted butter over a low heat for 5 minutes. Salt lightly, add freshly-ground black pepper and serve with butter sauce from pan	Very little vitamin C
Eggs 1 week, in cool, dark place, preferably not in the refrigerator			Protein. Vitamins A and D and B-group vitamins. Iron

Food	Storage	Best preparation	Source of
Fish Buy, cook and eat on the same day	Dry with kitchen paper towels before cooking. Use in any favourite recipes, retaining juices for sauces	Protein, vitamins A and B, and a little iron. Fatty fish such as kippers and salmon have vitamin D	
Grapefruit 3 to 5 days in refrigerator or cool place	Eat as a first course or add to salads. Try tossing it with chicory and orange segments or top with honey and grill [broil] for 5 minutes	Vitamin C	
Leeks 3 to 5 days in a refrigerator. 1 day loosely wrapped in paper in a cool, dark place	Cut off roots and tough outer leaves and wash well. Melt butter, add leeks and cook in covered pan for 5 to 10 minutes. Add salt and freshly ground black pepper. Use in soups and stews in place of onions	Some vitamin C	
Lemons 1 week in refrigerator	Squeeze and drink sweetened with brown sugar or use instead of vinegar in salad dressing	Vitamin C	
Lettuce Buy on the day required	Wash quickly under running water and dry thoroughly. Toss in vinaigrette dressing just before serving	A very little of vitamins A and C	
Meat 2 to 3 days covered in a refrigerator or buy on the day it is needed	Wipe with a damp cloth or kitchen paper before cooking. Use any recipe you like. Always use any juices that escape from the meat during cooking to make a sauce or gravy	Protein. Vitamin B group Liver and kidneys are exceptionally high in vitamin A and iron	
Melon 2 to 3 days when ripe	Eat sliced with no added sugar or dice and add to salads	A little of vitamins A and C	
Milk Do not leave exposed to light. Keep in refrigerator	Do not boil or keep hot for any length of time	Vitamins A and some B-group vitamins. Very rich in calcium	
Mushrooms Buy on the day they are needed	Wash thoroughly, but do not peel cultivated mushrooms. Trim stems. Try cooking for 20 minutes in aluminium foil parcel with pepper and lemon juice	Very little of the B-group vitamins	

59

Food	Storage	Best preparation	Source of
Onions 2 to 3 weeks loosely wrapped in paper in a cool, dark place. Do not refrigerate	Use peeled in soups and stews, roast with meat, steamed with cheese sauce or stuffed and baked	Very little vitamin C	
Oranges Keep 4 to 6 days	Eat freshly peeled whenever possible. Try adding to salads	High in vitamin C	
Parsley Wash and dry. Keep no longer than 3 to 6 days in a plastic container in refrigerator	Use as a garnish for salads, soups, sauces, meat and fish	Vitamin C and iron	
Peaches 2 to 3 days in a cool place when ripe	Eat raw	Vitamin A	
Pears 2 to 4 days when ripe	Eat raw or bake, tightly covered, in the oven for about 30 minutes with a little butter. Then pour on single [light] cream and serve immediately	Only a very little vitamin B. Calcium and iron	
Peas Buy and cook on same day of purchase	Shell and cook in chicken stock in a tightly covered dish in a moderate oven for 20 minutes	Some of the B-group vitamins and vitamin C	
Peppers Wash and dry. Keep in plastic bag in refrigerator for crispness	Eat raw, sliced in salads. Try baking them. If you add them to casseroles, first blanch for a moment in boiling water and then refresh by pouring cold water over them	Vitamin C and a little vitamin A	
Pineapple Buy and eat when ripe	Eat without sugar. Sprinkle·with a little liqueur for a change	A little of vitamins A and C. Small amount of vitamin B	
Potatoes Store in a dark place and never eat when they go green	Scrub well and bake in jackets. Eat potato in skin with butter for maximum nutritional value. Never peel potatoes and then leave them standing in cold water	Vitamin C and a very little vitamin B. Iron	

Food	Storage	Best preparation	Source of
Plums 2 to 3 days when ripe	Eat raw or stew gently with brown sugar in a tightly covered pan until just tender	Vitamin A
Raspberries Buy on day they are needed. Pick out bad or over-ripe fruit. Wash and dry before use	Eat as they are with cream and a little sugar if necessary	Rich in vitamin C
Spinach Buy on the day required	Wash leaves thoroughly. Place in a pan without water and cook, shaking, over very low heat for about 10 minutes. Drain and salt. Serve with melted butter and freshly ground black pepper	Vitamins A and C, calcium and iron
Spring onions [scallions] Keep 4 to 6 days in a plastic bag in the refrigerator	Use chopped in salads or as a garnish for stews and soups	Some vitamin C
Strawberries Buy on day they are needed. Pick out any bad or over-ripe fruit. Wash and dry before use	Eat as they are with cream or sprinkled with kirsch	Rich in vitamin C
Sweet Corn Buy on the day required and keep in plastic bag in refrigerator	Remove husk and "silk." Wash and cook in a little rapidly boiling water for 20 minutes. If cooked for too long, sweet corn becomes tough. Serve with melted butter and salt to taste.	Vitamin A and a little B
Tomatoes Buy when really firm and store in refrigerator	Use raw in salads. When soft can be used in soups and stews	Vitamins A and C
Turnips 3 to 4 days loosely covered in a cool, dark place	Wash, peel and use in soups and stews or steam and serve mashed with butter	Little vitamin C
Watercress Buy on day required	Wash thoroughly under running water. Use raw in salads and as a garnish for meat and fish. Also makes a delicious soup	Some of vitamins A and C and some iron and calcium

Keep the Flavour in Your Food

There's no doubt about it—good food does taste good. But what makes it taste good—or taste at all? It is a combination of many things, individual preferences and chemical reactions, how fresh the food is, how well it is prepared and cooked. Although it has a chemical basis, our sense of taste is very strongly affected by psychological factors, such as the look of a dish, or the associations that a particular food has for us.

Not all food sensations are taste sensations. The look of food is very important to the way we taste it; texture is also very important. Food can be smooth, soft, crisp, lumpy, thick, thin, coarse, fine, tough, tender, moist, dry, soggy, juicy, greasy and so on—these qualities are distinguished by pressure and touch sensations detected through muscular action in the mouth. And then there are sensations such as the burning effect of curry—if you have ever splashed a little curry sauce on to the skin round your eyes while cooking, you will know that the burning sensation is not one of taste, but of touch.

Temperature also affects the intensity of flavour of foods. Here again, foods are influenced in different ways. The taste of lemon tea, for example, grows more sour as it cools. At temperatures of over 100°F, or 38°C we lose the ability to detect salt and acid tastes, although the effect on sweet and bitter flavours is less pronounced. The aroma of many foods increases with heating, but keeping food hot once the aroma has been released is not a good idea, since the tantalizing fragrance may change or fade. Make a point of serving hot food hot, not lukewarm, and cold food properly chilled (but not frozen as this will destroy the flavour). If you are preparing food which is to be eaten cold or chilled, it is likely to need more seasoning than food which is to be served hot. But remember that, although sweet foods and wines become less sweet when chilled, saltiness increases as the temperature drops. If you want a really refreshing hot-weather taste, mint will exaggerate any degree of coolness picked up by the temperature receptors in the mouth.

The chemistry of taste works by dissolved substances in the food we eat coming into contact with sensitive cells. Quite different food can contain similar components—it is the blend of the various substances which gives a particular food its flavour.

But how exactly do we taste flavours? The tongue is the part of the mouth which directly picks up taste sensations through 'taste buds'—different parts of the tongue detect different flavours. Sweetness is sensed by the tip of the tongue, the front edges respond to saltiness, the edges further back to sourness or acidity and sensory receptors on the tongue grow less sensitive with age, so that flavours have to be relatively stronger.

Different flavours work together in different ways. Salt added to almost any food to bring out the flavour decreases the sourness of acids, but increases the sweetness of sugars. Adding a pinch of salt during preparation brings out the flavour of ice cream as it does of new potatoes. A salt-free diet, however carefully prepared, tends to be surprisingly dull.

Sugar reduces both saltiness and sourness, and a sweet pickle makes a good accompaniment to salty meat. In fruit, the sweetness of sugar and the sourness of the acids they contain combine to produce the pleasant refreshing taste. Many Chinese recipes combine sweet and sour flavours to tease the palate.

Bitterness, unlike sourness, is not counteracted by sugar. Bitterness magnifies sourness in foods. On its own it is a flavour which people naturally dislike. Most poisonous substances are bitter, and this aversion is part of the human instinct for self-preservation. Bitter flavours are more pronounced when foods are cold. Used sparingly, however, bitterness can be appetizing. This is why people often drink dry martinis before a meal—vermouth contains wormwood, which is very bitter.

But flavour is not just a question of chemical reactions. The cook who cares about food sets herself to bring out its finest flavours. She uses herbs to enhance its true taste, for example, not to mask the natural flavour. The thoughtful cook, the one who produces the best results, plans the seasonings and accompaniments to every dish she cooks and works out the best possible additions to bring out the flavour of tomatoes or pork, or whatever she happens to be cooking.

The same is true of sauces and other accompaniments. Good meat requires gravy or a sauce that complements its flavour, not a slushy, highly-flavoured sauce that drowns the taste of the meat. Blending flavours is not simply a question of 'the more the merrier'.

Cooking for flavour depends on the recognition that each food has its own character which you must bring out rather than drown. When you are planning a meal, think of the sequence of courses in relation to each other. Try and alternate bland and strong flavours, smooth and rough textures, heavy rich foods with light, refreshing ones. In this way you will get more out of the individual foods. Try to harmonize the colours of foods. Older meat very often has more taste than very young meat, so tougher and cheaper cuts can be a better buy, and the long slow cooking which they require will help the blending of flavours of other foods which you may add.

Other flavour-saving ways of cooking are dry-roasting in a chicken or fish 'brick', a specially shaped terra-cotta container, or cooking in foil or roasting bags. One good way of cooking chops or joints of poultry is to wrap each one in its own foil parcel with seasonings and accompaniments. You can then serve the food up in the parcels for each person to unwrap—that way the full aroma is released at the table. Make sure your casseroles have tightly-fitting lids—this will prevent the fragrance of the slowly-cooking ingredients from escaping.

When cooking, make sure you have at hand all the ingredients including the herbs, spices and other seasonings you need. Prepare them just before you are going to use them. Never soak salad ingredients or other vegetables in water—it will kill flavour just as surely as it destroys the nutrients—and for the same reason never overcook vegetables.

For maximum effect, pepper should be freshly ground as you need it. And the same applies to coffee—instant, and even the ground, vacuum-packed kind, are only poor substitutes for grinding the fresh beans every time you make coffee. You can buy a hand grinder quite cheaply if you cannot afford the electric sort, but whichever you use, the smell of the coffee beans as you grind them makes the extra effort thoroughly worthwhile.

Many cooks find that for special occasions—and sometimes for not-so-special occasions—wines and liqueurs with their own unique savours can add miraculously to the interest of a dish. The alcohol will evaporate during cooking and you will be left with all the carefully blended taste and fragrance of the wine. A miniature bottle of liqueur can be poured over a fruit salad or added to the whipped cream to be served with it. And sherry is not just for trifles—add it to consommé and sauces for an extra fillip.

Next time you cook, ask yourself whether you are using the food to its best advantage. If the answer is no, think what you could do to bring out the flavour or how you could complement it by adding other ingredients. Enjoy tasty food at every meal—it's easy when you know how!

Cooking for Flavour

Learn the art of enlivening your cooking without masking its true flavour. Read our suggestions for tastier food, and raid your cookery books (and those of your friends) for all sorts of possibilities. Some of the flavour combinations that work best may be the traditional ones—pork and apple, fish and lemon, turkey and cranberries, lamb and mint—which have been proved to work over the years. So don't discard the old ideas for the sake of it.

Try anything old or new—but note for next time what works and what doesn't. Your cooking will easily repay the little extra thought you give to it—a more imaginative approach can work wonders!

Think of a straightforward but pleasant menu:

Egg in mayonnaise with lettuce
garnish

Grilled [broiled] pork chop served
with tomatoes, mushrooms, peas and
sauté potatoes

Fresh fruit
Cheese

This would make a tasty and nourishing meal—but you could easily improve on it by serving a more exciting menu, such as:

Taramasalata
served with black and green olives
and hot toast and garnished with
lemon

Pork chops baked in sherry
with pickled prunes or walnuts
served with baked courgettes [zucchini]
and tomatoes and boiled new
potatoes with mint

Fresh orange and pineapple salad
with liqueur and thick cream

Selection of cheeses
with celery and sweet and plain
biscuits [crackers]

The second menu will certainly do more for your taste-buds, and it is simple to prepare. For taramasalata, soak white bread in olive oil and pound it smooth with smoked cod's roe, chopped onion, garlic, lemon juice and double [heavy] cream or cream cheese.

To cook the pork chops, brown them on both sides to seal in the flavour, place them in a baking dish with a glass of dry sherry, two tablespoons of stock or water and a few pickled prunes or walnuts. You then cover the dish with a lid or foil and bake the chops for 45 minutes to an hour at 325°F (Gas Mark 3).

Flavour Your Food

It's the nicest thing that you can do for your taste buds

BEEF

Traditional accompaniments are horse-radish sauce and mustard. Try serving roast beef with parsnips, vegetable marrow [summer squash], onions or carrots roasted in the baking tin. Serve steak with braised celery or chicory [endive]. Or sauté button onions and button mushrooms with chopped bacon, making a sauce by stirring red wine into the pan juices. Serve a traditional mustard sauce with cold beef. Marinade overnight in red wine, vegetables and spices, vinegar and oil before braising the beef. Or experiment with a carbonnade—a casserole made with beer and topped with slices of bread spread with mustard. When making meat balls, add sour cream or yogurt to the sauce.

VEAL

Flavour forcemeat stuffing for roast veal with thyme, tarragon or rosemary. Serve rolls of bacon as an accompaniment, or try orange slices for a change.

PORK

Minimize the richness by serving with baked apples, pickled prunes or walnuts, apricots and orange slices. Press a few cloves into the outer edge of a chop or a joint before cooking. Rub the surface with sage or thyme, or try brushing a joint with honey before roasting it.

LAMB AND MUTTON

Roast lamb on a bed or fresh rosemary. Make slits in the outside of a joint before roasting and insert slivers of garlic. Serve Greek-style kebabs with marjoram and slices of lemon. Try a mutton stew with onion or caper sauce, or cook with fennel—this counteracts the fat.

CHICKEN

Tarragon goes exceptionally well with chicken. Make coq au vin (chicken casserole with red wine) for a special occasion. Stuff roasting chicken with either apples, celery, mushrooms or sweet chestnuts.

TURKEY

Serve with chestnut stuffing. Cook turkey joints in cider.

DUCK

Flavour orange sauce with Madeira wine or sherry. Stuff with soaked and drained dried apricots flavoured with cinnamon.

FISH

Garnish fish with shrimps, mushrooms or orange slices as well as lemon. Serve cooked fish with a border of piped mashed potato browned in the oven. Or cover the fish with mornay sauce, sprinkle with grated cheese and melt the cheese under the grill [broiler] until it is golden brown and bubbly. You can make special bouquets garnis for fish, by putting some herbs such as parsley, bayleaf, thyme, celery, chervil, tarragon and fennel in small muslin bags which you can suspend in a fish casserole while it is cooking. Experiment with savoury butters—garlic, anchovy, tarragon, parsley or shrimp.

VEGETABLES

Steamed or boiled vegetables always taste nicer with a knob of butter and freshly-ground black pepper. Mashed or duchesse potatoes taste better with a little grated horseradish root, if you can get it. Add a little sugar when you cook peas and carrots, and when you make the dressing for a tomato salad. Add fresh herbs to salads and salad dressings. Try some new ways with baked potatoes—scoop out the centres and mix with smoked haddock, grated cheese, cooked minced [ground] beef, sour cream, yogurt or hard-boiled egg.

FRUITS

Judicious use of liqueurs can transform stewed fruit. Try adding orange liqueur to orange slices and simmering them in sugar-and-water syrup. Bake pears in cider. Stuff peaches with chopped almonds, or try sprinkling them with dried ginger. It goes just as well with peaches as it does with melon.

10 Ways to Tasty Food...

1. Experiment with different flavour combinations
2. Plan your menus—one strong flavour per meal is usually enough
3. Make full use of casserole cookery—it's a marvellous way of blending tastes
4. Season your food with freshly ground black pepper (add at the end of cooking) and sea salt
5. Use strong flavours sparingly, except for special effect
6. Balance the colour and texture of dishes
7. Always adjust seasonings a few moments before serving any dish
8. Try foil cookery—it stops fragrance and flavour escaping during cooking
9. Use all foods as fresh as possible—taste and nutritional value both decrease with storage and exposure to air
10. Remember that convenience foods could often do with extra flavour, such as a sprinkling of herbs, a spoonful of tomato purée, or a handful of chopped nuts

...and 5 Things to Avoid

1. Don't rush either cooking or eating—give yourself time to enjoy it
2. Avoid overcooking food—green vegetables become strong and bitter-flavoured, meat gets tough and dry
3. Resist the temptation to throw in handfuls of herbs regardless—everything you cook will end up tasting the same
4. Don't spurn traditional flavourings and accompaniments
5. Don't be lazy about leftovers—there are all sorts of imaginative ways to use them up

The Need for Salt

Everyone takes salt very much for granted, treating it as an "optional extra". We use vague quantities in cooking and sprinkle it with gay abandon over our food. But why use salt at all?

Imagine yourself eating a boiled egg. First you dip your bread and butter "soldier" into the yolk and then into the pile of salt on the side of the plate. In your mouth, the salt crystals start to dissolve immediately on your tongue and to titillate your taste buds. Then gradually the full eggy flavour comes through for you to savour. The salt helps to lift the rather bland taste of the egg and bring out a strong eggy taste.

In fact, salt is used very widely to enhance the natural flavours of foods. You may sprinkle salt over everything you eat before even tasting it just because you know from experience that you like your food to taste salty or simply because you like the feel of the crystals and the contrast between very salty and unsalted bits of food in your mouth. Or you may use salt sparingly and always test your food first and then pour a small pile of salt on the side of your plate.

Cooks, too, vary in their use of salt. In general the British cook uses little or no salt, leaving the person who eats the food to add it at the table. The American cook tends to add salt during the cooking. In all cases you are using salt to improve the flavour and hence your enjoyment of your food.

Most foods contain some salt anyway but the amounts occuring naturally in them contribute less to the average diet than that added during cooking, at the table or in processing and preserving foods. Foods such as bread, biscuits, cornflakes, canned vegetables, corned beef, ham, bacon, sausages, canned and cured fish, cheese, salted butter and margarine and bottled sauces contain significant amounts of salt. But foods such as flour, rice, shredded wheat, sugar, unsalted nuts, fruits, fruit juices, lard, unsalted butter and margarine and oil contain comparatively little salt.

Salt is also an important and ancient method of preserving food. It dissolves readily in the cells of the food to give a concentrated salt solution. Micro-organisms, normally responsible for decomposition and spoilage of the food, are killed in the strong salt mixture and preservation is effected. Many salted foods are also smoked but the salting, which usually precedes smoking, is the most important preserving agent. The substances formed by smoke are only mildly preservative. Heavily salted and then smoked foods do have a longer storage life than slightly salted ones.

So salt is invaluable as a seasoning and preserving agent. But how important is the salt in our diets? What part does it play in our bodies and does it matter how much or how little we eat?

Salt, or sodium chloride, is essential to life. It is vital for good health that the concentration of salt in the blood and other body fluids should be maintained within quite narrow limits. Our kidneys play the most important part in regulat-

Salt is essential to life. But just what use does your body make of the salt that you sprinkle in your cooking and over your food ?

ing the level of salt in the body. Hormones secreted by the adrenal glands control this aspect of kidney function. When too much salt is eaten, the kidneys excrete a salty urine. When salt levels are low, the kidneys conserve salt and in some cases there may be no salt at all in the urine.

It is difficult to estimate how much salt an individual needs each day as losses via the kidneys, sweat and tears vary widely. An average daily loss is generally given as four grams a day, while an average daily intake is usually between five and 12 grams. If a person has healthy kidneys, it does not matter if he eats more salt than his body requires that day, for the surplus will simply be excreted in the urine.

Sometimes, you may feel very thirsty after eating a salty meal and drink large quantities of liquid to quench your thirst. This is another way in which your body compensates for the extra salt. In a similar way, ship-wrecked sailors are exposed to the danger of having too much salt. The Ancient Mariner, in Coleridge's poem, knew this all too well when he cried, "Water, water everywhere. Nor any drop to drink." Sea-water has a salt concentration of 2.9 per cent in arctic waters and 3.55 per cent and upwards near the tropics as opposed to the 0.9 per cent of body fluids. Although it is the job of the kidneys to get rid of any excess salt in urine, there is a limit to their capacity. Drinking sea-water can soon increase the concentration of salt in the body to these limits with such tragic results as dehydration of the cells and even death.

Because salt retention is usually accompanied by water retention, people on slimming diets sometimes think that they should restrict their salt intake. There is no evidence that this is a sound practice except when there is some serious disease in addition to the over-weight problem. The amount of water retained by taking ordinary amounts of salt is small compared with the amount of fat which is what the slimmer should be concerned with. Nor is there any evidence to suggest that excess salt and water can lead to an increase in body fat.

On the other hand, the treatment of some medical conditions, such as congestive heart failure and cirrhosis of the liver, frequently includes some restriction of salt in the diet, particularly of the very salty foods, and addition of salt at the table. Salt restriction is also sometimes prescribed for people who suffer from severe hypertension (high blood pressure) on the assumption that reducing the salt in the blood also reduces the amount of water circulating, and thus the volume of blood and the pressure in the blood vessels.

In contrast to having a surfeit of salt in the diet, there are the problems of excessive salt loss. Every time you shed a tear, work up a good sweat or go to the toilet, you lose some salt from your body. And salt levels can become dangerously low during certain illnesses, especially those where there is prolonged vomiting, sweating due to fever, diarrhoea or a large loss of blood. When the salt concentration is really low there is usually an accompanying loss of water and a reduced volume of blood leading to low blood pressure. This produces some unpleasant symptoms such as mental apathy, vomiting, and finally severe muscle cramps, which all leave a person feeling tired and weak.

Great salt loss is always a potential danger to health for people working in hot conditions, such as coal miners or steel workers, or living and working in hot climates, which cause profuse sweating. Sweating is the body's mechanism for bringing down its temperature, because the evaporation of moisture from the skin produces a cooling effect. But with the water in sweat, there is also a large salt loss. The loss of salt and water

and the failure to replenish them can be a cause of the tired, listless feeling experienced by many people living under such conditions. Even worse, these losses can lead to heat exhaustion.

People at risk are usually advised to increase the amount of salt they add to food in cooking and at the table and to drink plenty of water. This need is likely to be greatest when people first experience very hot conditions. Later, when the body has adapted to such conditions, salt is conserved by excreting a more dilute sweat. Even so, it is wise to take extra salt and water, as neither thirst nor a craving for salt are necessarily reliable guides to requirements.

The obvious solution to excessive salt loss is to eat more salt, but it is not as simple as that. A large salt loss is practically always accompanied by a large loss of water. Just think back to the last time you got hot enough to sweat profusely and recall how wet your clothes became.

Fluid lost in sweating contains salt. But if you just replace the lost salt without the water, then the concentration of salt in body fluids can become too high. When this happens, vital water is withdrawn from the body cells in an effort to dilute the salt in the fluids and bring them back to normal concentrations and so the cells become dehydrated. The reverse happens when large amounts of water are drunk without replacing the salt. This condition, when the cells absorb water instead of becoming dehydrated, is known as water intoxication.

The safest way to replenish salt is either to use well-salted food and drink lots of water, or to drink a weak salt solution, or to take salt tablets with a prescribed amount of water. A recommended weak salt solution, containing about five per cent salt, is a mixture of 1 level teaspoon of salt to 20 fluid ounces of water. This is quite pleasant to drink if well chilled, and can be a wonderful pick-me-up after strenuous exercise in hot conditions.

Exactly why humans crave salt in their food, over and above the needs of their bodies, is obscure. Anthropologists know that in many parts of the world primitive man was probably unable to obtain salt,

and there are still many people in the world who never use salt. Their bodies rely on the quantities of salt that occur naturally in their food.

There is no evidence that humans living on a diet containing animal foods such as milk and meat, need any added salt, especially if they cook the meat by roasting or other methods which retain the juices. On the other hand, people who live largely on cereals and vegetables need salt, as these foods contain only small amounts, which can be lost when the foods are boiled. Possibly man's need for and craving for salt is connected with the change from man as a hunter largely,

Just as a boiled egg needs salt to make it taste eggy, so other foods need salt to bring out and enhance their full, natural flavours.

living on animals, to man as an agriculturist, practising crop cultivation.

Some authorities attribute the fact that man craves salt over and above his physiological needs to some emotional effect. It could also be habit and might even have its roots in snobbery. When salt was scarce and expensive, to be seated at table above the position of the ornamental salt cellar showed you had made the social grade.

Contrary to popular opinion, there is no evidence that one kind of salt is better for you than another. All domestic supplies of salt come originally from the sea. Much of the world's salt is obtained simply by the evaporation of salt water, either naturally, due to the heat of the sun (solar evaporation), or, in colder climates, by artificial heating.

Crystalline salt occurs in rock deposits in many parts of the world. The oldest known salt mine has been found in the Austrian Tyrol and dates from the late Bronze age, about 1,000 B.C. In Britain, the Cheshire mines were known at the time of Roman occupation, although the mines have been worked only since the seventeenth century. North America and Europe are leaders in the modern method of extracting salt from rock deposits by making bores, filling them with water,

then pumping out the brine to evaporate it.

Table salt is 91 to 96 per cent pure sodium chloride with various other chemical compounds of potassium, magnesium, calcium and other minerals. The amounts of these are small compared with the amounts of the same minerals in normal foods, so in this respect their presence in salt makes an insignificant contribution to the diet. During the evaporation of brine to make salt, a proportion of these compounds, other than sodium chloride, are removed. Health-food and "whole-food" enthusiasts oppose this and favour "sea" salt, which contains larger amounts of chemicals in addition to sodium chloride. They claim these are beneficial to health, particularly the potassium compounds.

Potassium is as important to life as sodium and a balance between sodium and potassium in the body is important, but practically all foods contain potassium, usually in much larger amounts than the 30.55 per cent sodium to 1.11 per cent potassium that occur in seawater. Plant foods, such as wholemeal flour, have 100 times more potassium than sodium. The justification for eating "sea" salt is that you prefer the taste and feel of its coarser texture.

Iodised salt is a different matter. This is ordinary salt with iodine added. Seawater contains only traces of iodine. Iodised salt has proved to be an important means of supplying extra iodine to control goitre, a thyroid condition, in parts of the world where iodine is lacking in the local soil and drinking water and in locally-grown food plants.

Salt is, indeed, a most important item in our diet. There are obviously many factors influencing individual requirements. Whether it matters how much or how little we add to our food depends on such variables as climate, physical activity, and the individual's state of health. But for the average sedentary or moderately active person, with a healthy pair of kidneys, living in a temperate climate, eating a mixed diet of animal and vegetable foods, the evidence suggests that it doesn't matter if salt is a food taken for granted and used merely to suit individual tastes.

Spices and Seasonings

Anyone who has tried to keep to a diet knows that one of the main obstacles to success is boredom. But it's not the actual proteins, vitamins and minerals of a well-balanced diet that become tedious. The sense of taste is not even aware of their existence. What it is aware of is *flavour*, and when it grows too accustomed to certain ones, it almost ceases to register them. When any combination of foods—however balanced or nutritious—becomes tasteless, its dullness makes it unappetizing.

In its working taste is the most mysterious of the five senses. Sight, hearing and touch work independently of one another, but there are very few tastes which are not basically smells. The true tastes, those which are detected by the mouth alone, are sourness, bitterness,

sharpness, sweetness, chalky and metallic flavours, and those that are strong and pungent to the point of being uncomfortable.

A good diet is not simply a set pattern of nutritious, well-balanced meals. It involves eating food that interests and pleases your nose and your palate. The best diet does not taste precisely the same, day after day. On the contrary, if it provides an intriguing variety of flavours and scents, it will cease to be a test of perseverance and become what it should always be—the kind of food you can enjoy preparing and eating.

In many diets, a baked apple is a staple dessert. And for a time, it is a pleasant dish to eat, just as it is. The hot fruit is light and fluffy, and the taste, the winey sharpness, is refreshing. But the taste is

NUTMEG　　TURMERIC　　CINNAMON

almost entirely a true one, detected by the mouth alone. The scent of the cooked fruit is very faint indeed. So, something that was pleasing to eat at first becomes dull because it lacks any interest for the sense of taste. But a baked apple with a clove, or a fragment of cinnamon stick in its hollowed-out centre smells and tastes delicious. Its value in calories or carbohydrates has not increased. All that has happened is that a very small amount of spice has changed a dull dish into one which can be savoured while it's still cooking and thoroughly enjoyed when the time comes to eat it.

Because spices have this power to stimulate and intrigue the senses of smell and taste, they have been sought after and valued for thousands of years. In the distant past, their use was often a matter of sheer necessity, too—they did not make up for a lack of taste or aroma, but disguised strong and unpleasant ones. Before there was any form of cold storage, much food had to be eaten when it was 'off'. Meat and fish could be salted for preservation, but this made for a monotonous and unappetizing diet, particularly in the winter months. With spices the smell and taste of unwholesome or dull food could be masked. But this use only accounted for a part of their value. It was chiefly based on the great pleasure which spices added to eating. They had a high value, too, just because they were exotic. Only wealthy people could afford them: poorer people used herbs which they could gather for themselves for flavouring. The old records of recipes and household budgets that have survived almost always deal with meals which were prepared and enjoyed in well-to-do, and sometimes royal, houses—the homes of people for whom spices were a necessary luxury.

They were costly mainly because they had to be imported from far-off countries. The spice routes from the Orient crossed vast distances through many lands, where the terrain and the climate made difficulties and dangers. The spice caravans had to survive these natural hazards and ambush and robbery, too. As a consequence, the spice traders wanted profit for the hardships they risked or endured. And rivalry among European countries caused enmity and bloodshed.

Today, spices are no longer a cause of international wrangling, but they can still be costly in the literal sense. The

CAPSICUM   MACE   MUSTARD

world supply of **cloves,** for example, comes from Zanzibar, and if the crop fails, the price rises. However, even if that does happen, cloves are economical to buy, for a small quantity will last for a long time, and stay in good condition. This is particularly true of whole cloves, which should look shapely, plump and oily when you buy them, not shrivelled and dusty. But ground cloves can be stored, too, and will keep their aroma.

This is strong and very definite and so cloves—like every other spice—should always be used sparingly. A spice is, after all, an addition to a dish. It should combine with whatever flavour the food already has in itself, not obliterate it. A baked apple tasting of nothing but cloves is no more interesting than one tasting of nothing but apple. It is the combination between the sharpness of the fruit and the soft, warm taste of the spice that is so pleasant. It is helpful to use a definite amount of any spice until you find out how strong you like its taste to be. Count how many whole cloves you put into a particular dish. Measure out the amount of a ground spice in a very small spoon—as small as a salt spoon, for example. When you are eating a dish which you have spiced, you can soon decide whether the flavour is strong enough. And the process of cooking has an effect on the strength of the spice in the food. One clove in a casserole of beef, cooked slowly and gently in a dish with a tight-fitting lid, will not taste at all, but it will give its aroma to the meat, and consequently improve the whole casserole.

Allspice is mild in flavour and this makes it particularly useful in the kitchen. Its name suggests that it is a mixture of many spices, but in fact it is the berry of an evergreen member of the myrtle family. Its scent, however, is a combination of clove, cinnamon and nutmeg, and this gives it versatility. It is best bought whole and ground when it is needed in a pepper-mill kept especially for the purpose. When you first begin to use it, think of the taste of a fresh, spiced bun: with the flavour of allspice in your memory, you will be able to judge whether you want it to be very definitely present in what you are cooking, or subdued and in the background.

A spice whose flavour is very hard to subdue is **ginger.** It makes a strong and immediate impression on the taste buds, but it doesn't have to be uncomfortably

hot. Powdered Jamaican ginger is finer and more delicately flavoured than either Chinese or African ginger. Try using a very little of it, shaken on a well-chilled slice of melon or fresh pineapple, and enjoy the delicious blend of flavours and the curious balance of hot and cold.

Mustard is also generally thought of as a very hot spice, but the many varieties of it vary distinctly in flavour from one another. French mustard, more delicate and aromatic than English mustard, comes mainly from the Dijon area. It has been made there for over six hundred years—one Dijon mustard blender is said to have invented over ninety varieties. English mustard has a clean, vivid taste. Its pungency is due to an oil which forms when the powder is mixed with water. This does not happen immediately, and English mustard is tastiest when the powder has been mixed with cold water into a smooth, silky paste and allowed to stand for about ten minutes. American mustard is mellower and comes somewhere between English and French in flavour. Cooking destroys some of the flavour in mustard, and so it is best to add it late to a dish and to cook it gently.

Cardamom is a member of the ginger family. The seed pods appear slowly and at different times, and are either dried (by sun or artificial heat) or bleached white. Since cardamom is one of the more expensive spices, it is well worth making sure that it is in good condition when you buy it. The seeds inside the pod should be sticky, brownish-black in colour and with a distinctive flavour, a little like eucalyptus. If the seeds are ground, the oils which give cardamom this characteristic taste and smell are lost, so it is best to buy them in the pod.

Some spices sound exotic, simply by their name—cardamom is one of them. Nutmeg, cinnamon and pepper are much more familiar, and because they tend to be associated with certain set uses, their versatility is often forgotten, or at any rate, not enjoyed to the full. Nutmeg and cinnamom are not simply 'cake spices' and pepper has a life of its own, quite apart from being teamed with salt.

Nutmeg had reached Europe by the twelfth century but could not be had in any quantity until Portugal discovered the Spice Islands in 1512. Thereafter it became a favourite spice. A ruler of Persia in the eighteenth century described himself as 'the nutmeg of delight'. People often carried their own pocket nutmeg graters with them when they travelled, so that they could be sure of having the spice on their food and in mulled wine or ale. Kitchen spice boxes, too, generally had a little circular box inside them, large enough to contain a nutmeg and grater. It is best to follow tradition and grate nutmeg as you need it. Ground nutmeg loses its aroma quickly.

Nutmeg is at its best, perhaps, when

its flavour is half-submerged in some other equally definite flavour. It is a delicious addition to cheese or onion sauce, for example, and goes well with cream cheese or with spinach. **Cinnamon,** like nutmeg, used to be used very much as a condiment. A great many English households, for example, owned a cinnamon caster and very much enjoyed the spice sprinkled on hot toast or muffins. It is easier to use in its finely ground form, rather than in sticks, and it is at its most delicious when it is very fresh. Buy it frequently, store it in a bottle or jar with a well-fitting top, and use it up quickly.

Ground **pepper,** like ground nutmeg, soon deteriorates. Some of the inferior brands of ground pepper may also be adulterated with other poor quality spices, or crushed date stones. Anyone who knows it only in this powdered form will have the great pleasure of discovering the taste and scent of freshly-ground pepper. Choose peppercorns that are of even size, large and black—too hard to crush between the finger nails, and free of stalks or dust. These are often part of the mixture in inferior ready-ground pepper, one reason why it produces a prickly, uncomfortable feeling in the mouth, with none of the aroma and taste of freshly-ground pepper.

This contains an alkaloid which makes the saliva and the gastric juices flow, and so it helps digestion. In cooking it keeps its scent but its flavour loses strength, so if you like the 'bite' of pepper in the mouth as well as its smell, add it at the end of the cooking time. Pepper ground from white peppercorns is much hotter than that ground from the black variety. If you want to create your own special blend of aroma and flavour, grind white and black peppercorns together in the same mill and make 'mignonette pepper' according to the French method.

This is the third great pleasure which spices provide. As well as the delight of their flavour and scent, they make cooking interesting, creative, a genuine expression of individuality. Recipes often use the phrase 'flavour to taste' and that can seem an irritatingly useless instruction if you are about to use cinnamon, say, for the first time. But one of the pleasantest things about cooking is that it can never be turned into an exact science. No cookery writer, however knowledgeable, could possibly tell you exactly how much to use of allspice or cinnamon or mustard or any other spice. You discover this, as every experienced cook has done, by experiment. At the beginning of discovery, it is wise to make simple spiced dishes and just enough of them for you to eat by yourself. A meal which other people are going to share is obviously not a good occasion for experiment. Once you have discovered how much pleasure spices add to food, you will have found out, too, how to use them skilfully. The two discoveries go together.

ALLSPICE

Spiced Beetroot [beet] Salad
Remove the skin of a freshly-cooked beetroot of medium size. Cut it into cubes and season with salt and ground allspice. Make a little oil-and-wine-vinegar dressing and add this to the beetroot, together with some chopped parsley. (Allspice is a particularly delicious seasoning for hot beetroot.)
Spiced Grapefruit
Halve a grapefruit and separate the segments with a sharp knife. Spread butter very sparingly on top of the fruit and sprinkle it with allspice and a little brown sugar. Heat the grapefruit for about 5 minutes under the grill [broiler] or in a hot oven.

CINNAMON

Cheese and Plum Salad
1 lb. ripe eating plums
4 oz. [1 cup] **finely grated Cheddar cheese**
2 **level teaspoons mayonnaise generous pinch of cinnamon lettuce leaves and a little watercress**
After washing and drying the plums, cut them in half and remove the stones. Mix the grated cheese, mayonnaise and cinnamon into a soft paste, shape this into small balls and put one in each plum, so that it forms a 'sandwich filling' between the two halves of the fruit. Arrange the plums on the lettuce leaves and decorate with watercress.
A variation—Cheese and Apple Ring Salad
Remove the cores from two or three medium-sized eating apples, but do not peel them. Cut the apples into thick slices, with the hole left by the removal of the core in the centre of them. Sprinkle the apple slices well with fresh lemon juice. Arrange a ball of spiced cheese in the centre of each of them and decorate it with a walnut. Stand the apple slices on a bed of lettuce leaves.

Cinnamon Toast (for non-weight-watchers)
Make toast in the ordinary way. Remove crusts, and cut the slices of toast into fingers. Butter them while they are still hot and sprinkle them with cinnamon and sugar.

GINGER

Gooseberry and Ginger Sauce
Remove the tops and tails from 1 lb. of gooseberries. Wash well. Just cover the fruit with cold water and cook gently until tender. Sweeten according to taste. Sieve the cooked fruit (or mash it very thoroughly) and add a little powdered ginger. Serve the gooseberry sauce hot. (It is excellent with baked mackerel.)
Grapefruit and Ginger
Halve a grapefruit and separate the segments with a sharp knife. Into the spaces between the segments put thin slices of preserved ginger. Spread a little of the syrup in which the ginger was preserved on top of the grapefruit and heat the fruit

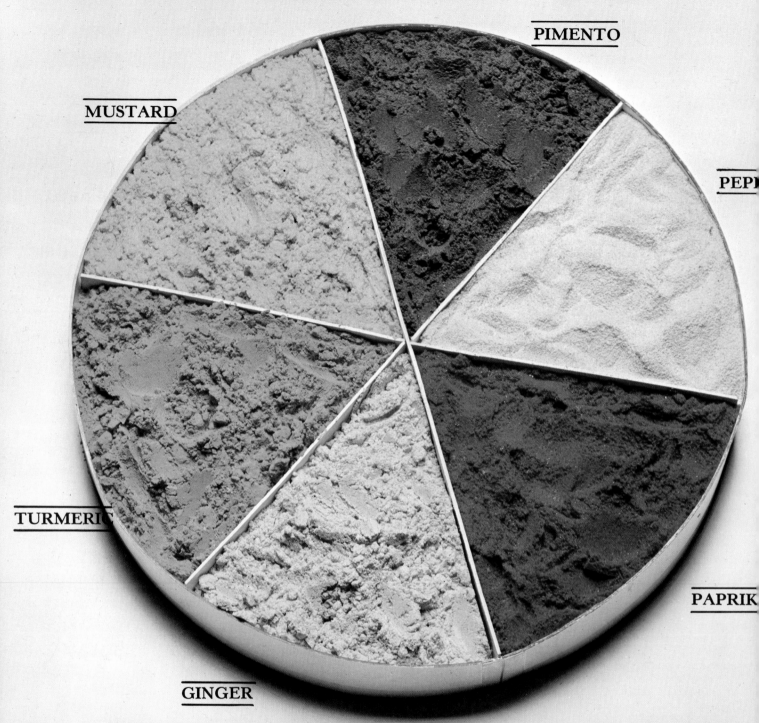

PIMENTO

MUSTARD

PEP[

PEPPER

TURMERIC

PAPRIK

PAPRIKA

GINGER

under the grill [broiler] or in a hot oven, for about 5 minutes.

MUSTARD

Russian Mustard Sauce
  3 egg yolks
  2 tablespoons olive oil
  2 tablespoons wine vinegar
  1 tablespoon chopped olives
  1 teaspoon made English mustard
Mix the yolks and the mustard together thoroughly with a wooden spoon. Add the oil slowly. Keep beating until the oil is all used and the mixture thickens. Dilute it gradually with the vinegar. Add the chopped olives. Sweeten slightly to taste.
(The sauce is excellent with some cold fish—halibut, for example).

NUTMEG

Baked Bananas
Peel the bananas and split them lengthways, then cut the two pieces into halves. Melt a little butter in a baking dish. Put the pieces of banana into the dish. Squeeze the juice of a lemon and an orange over them. Add a little soft brown sugar, nutmeg and cinnamon. Arrange strips of lemon peel on top of the bananas and bake for about thirty minutes in a moderate oven.

CLOVES

Spiced Cheese
  a carton of cottage cheese or about $\frac{1}{2}$ lb. of cream cheese

$\frac{1}{4}$ **teaspoon each of ground cloves, freshly-grated nutmeg and salt**
Work the spices and the salt well into the cheese. If the mixture is stiff, add a little milk, and sweeten it slightly, according to taste. Spiced cheese goes well with apricots. Soak dried apricot rings overnight, then stew them very gently until they are plump, using the liquid in which they have been soaking, and cooking them in a pan with a well-fitting lid. Serve them hot or cold with the spiced cheese.

CARDAMOM

A flavouring for fresh coffee
Put an opened pod of cardamom seeds into the spout of the coffee pot, so that the coffee absorbs the flavour of the spice as it is poured out.

What About Health Food?

Throughout the West health-food shops and restaurants are springing up. They cater to a small but rapidly growing group of people who come from all walks of life, and range from teenagers to the elderly. But what is the difference between the food on sale in health-food shops and that which most of us eat?

A health food quite simply preserves so far as possible the whole nutritional complex of natural ingredients and thereby reduces the need for chemical additives. Synthetic flavours, artificial colourings and preservatives are avoided whenever possible. But every time the average person goes into a supermarket, food shop or restaurant he chooses and selects foods which he believes will keep him fit and healthy.

The selection which confronts him, however, is bewilderingly complex. And in today's prosperous society, where most of us have enough to eat, everyone is beginning increasingly to question their choice, focussing their attention on the quality of the food they eat and the ways in which it is produced.

The food eaten by primitive men was natural in a way that food no longer can be. Agricultural and food experts believe that it would not be possible to produce enough food to feed the ever increasing world population if only natural compost and manure fertilizers were used. Not only would food production decrease, but the high unit cost of natural foods for world-wide distribution would be prohibitive.

Over the years our bodies have learned to cope with the naturally occurring toxic substances in food. But during the past 50 years, and particularly in the last 15 years, there has been a tremendous increase in the number of man-made additives both to food and to the soil. Today about 3,000 additives are used in foods, compared with about 100 at the beginning of the twentieth century.

Many nutritionists are satisfied that government-imposed regulations on food additives are adequate. They believe that chemical fertilizers and synthetics are not at levels that might endanger health. They claim that foods processed or prepared entirely without the use of additives are highly likely to deteriorate or change with time, resulting in loss of nutrients.

Health-food enthusiasts, on the other hand, argue that modern methods of food processing, especially in the canning and freezing of foods where chemical preservatives are added, result in considerable loss of natural nutrients. They believe that these are potentially harmful or have not been proven harmless.

In a health-food diet, unpolished rice, for example, which retains the B vitamins, is preferred. Raw sugar and sea salt in moderation replace their refined counterparts. Flour is made from the whole grain. Fruit and vegetables are grown without chemicals. If a preservative has to be used, for example to stop cider vinegar from moulding, a natural one, such as vitamin C (ascorbic acid) is usually chosen.

Advocates of health foods prefer wholemeal stone-ground bread to white or even brown bread. The loaf must contain 100 per cent of the wheat grain, which may be a better source than white bread of some of the vitamins of the B group such as riboflavin. The white loaf has no traces of chromium, an element believed to be of importance in building blood cells. White flour contains 9.8 per cent protein while wholemeal flour contains 11.9 per cent as well as less carbohydrate, 71.2 per cent as compared to 77 per cent.

We must learn to choose and prepare food so that it will keep us fit and healthy. We must look before we eat.

Stone-grinding generates a degree of heat which stabilizes and disperses the wheat-germ oil, a valuable source of vitamin E, binding it to the flour so that it is not lost. This binding affects the flavouring components of the flour. Bread baked from stone-ground wheat has an identifiably individual flavour. There is no waste of natural nutrients and therefore it is unnecessary to fortify it artificially.

Commercial white bread, on the other hand, is artificially enriched. Many of the micronutrients which are lost in the milling and refining of the wheat are restored in accordance with government specifications. However, the bran which is retained in wholewheat bread is absent from white bread. The only significant difference is one of individual preference for natural rather than synthetic vitamins.

Sea salt, too, is part of a health-food diet. In addition to the sodium chloride of common salt, sea salt contains magnesium, potassium, bromine and iodine. In controlled laboratory experiments it was found that a diet high in salt produced in rats a 50 per cent incidence of raised blood pressure. Adding potassium, it was discovered, minimizes this problem. Sea salt, which contains potassium, and so has a natural safety factor absent from common salt, has a firm place in any diet, in small amounts.

Although natural sugar is preferred, there is no way to consume it apart from honey or, perhaps, cane sugar. Raw sugar, not just coloured white sugar but a real raw product, provides minerals which are missing from processed sugar and, more important, you cannot easily eat as much. Natural sugar is quickly assimilated into the body, and can be used at once for energy production. Honey can be substituted for processed sugars in tea and coffee, and it can also be used in cooking as a sweetener. But raw sugars are not lower in calories than processed sugars.

In promoting the use of vegetable rather than animal fats, health-food advocates have the strong backing of medical evidence. Researchers confirm that some fats and oils are high in essential fatty acids, vital to human nutrition, while others are deficient. The only animal fats that are rich in these essential fatty acids are fish oils and these certainly cannot be used for cooking, frying or salads.

The best vegetable oils include corn, soya, safflower, sunflower and olive oils. Margarine, which is fortified with the natural vitamin A found in fish oils, is an exception, where an essentially artificial product based on vegetable oil has advantages over the natural animal fat equivalent—butter.

Many doctors believe that a high incidence of cholesterol in the blood is a significant factor in causing and aggravating heart disease. It is known that while animals fats raise this cholesterol level, vegetable fats lower it. But health food shops do not have to be relied upon for vegetable oils. Corn oil, for example, is widely available.

Recent articles in the British Medical Journal have stated that certain of modern civilization's illnesses are caused by man's

reliance on refined foods. The rough cereal fibre in the bran, for example, which is retained in wholemeal bread is known to play a vital role in the working of the body.

The newcomer to the health-food scene can be forgiven for becoming confused about the many and various health-food sub-groups who push their points of view with a fervour of theological intensity. There are, first, those people who eat only wholefoods.

Wholefoods are foods grown in as near ideal conditions as possible. Sprays and artificial fertilizers are not used, or only minimally so. Compost is returned to the soil and the use of artificial fertilizers is frowned upon. Animals are produced for meat and for dairy foods on the same basis. Chickens are allowed to run free and have neither antibiotics nor hormone injections.

Produce must be eaten or converted into foods when it is in the peak of condition. It must be prepared in a way that will conserve nutritional advantages. As the name implies, whenever possible the whole food, such as brown rice and wholemeal flour, is used.

Second are vegetarians, who do not eat meat. There are some vegetarians, however, who do eat fish, but will not consume warm-blooded animals. The vegetarian must choose and balance his diet with care and knowledge so that he ensures an adequate intake of protein.

Vegans take the vegetarian principle one step further. They eat no meat, nor such animal products as butter, milk or cheese because they believe that this is an exploitation of a fellow creature. This is difficult from the protein point of view, especially for young and growing children, but a vegan can be healthy.

Macrobiotics is a diet based on brown rice which, it is said, creates an effective balance of "yin" and "yang," of acidity and alkalinity, for the individual. Meat is considered a secondary food. Fruits are "yin" and most cereals are "yang."

Adherence to the more extreme aspects of this diet can result in malnutrition.

Health-food enthusiasts stock their kitchens with wheat germ, wholemeal flour, cider vinegar, sea salt, wholegrain macaroni, brown rice, honey, dried skimmed milk, powdered brewer's yeast, dandelion coffee, raisins, figs, dates, sesame-seed oil, sunflower-seed oil, a variety of herbs, China and herb teas and nuts.

But you can eat healthful food without restocking your kitchen or reorganizing your life around the foods you eat. All that is necessary is some knowledge of nutrition combined with common sense. When you go into a food store, for example, compare the list of ingredients on food labels. Read the contents and choose the purest and most natural foods.

Include fresh fruit, vegetables, milk and wholemeal bread in your diet and increase the variety of the proteins you eat with cottage cheese, nuts, especially hazelnuts, walnuts and peanuts, eggs, fresh meat and fish, beans and lentils.

Health foods preserve their natural nutrients and so they reduce the need for any chemical additives.

Try using yogurt with fruit salads instead of cream. Slice washed, fresh fruit and mix with yogurt. This makes a different and nutritious breakfast, which provides calcium and vitamins of the B complex.

Use vegetable oils as a base for salad dressings. Try new, subtle combinations of tastes, such as sunflower-seed oil, sea salt, paprika and lemon juice. Yogurt, a teaspoon of orange juice and orange rind goes well with raw, grated cabbage. Cider vinegar, honey and garlic will enhance a crisp green salad.

Eat ripe, raw fruit at every meal. Wash it well and, where possible, eat it with the skin. Peeling the skin from fruits and vegetables also peels away a high proportion of vitamins and minerals. If you are hungry between meals, nibble on a carrot, a pear or an apple instead of biscuits or chocolate. Keep a supply of dried fruit in your desk drawer.

When preparing vegetables, wash but do not soak them. Vegetables should always be dropped into fast boiling water. Steam helps to seal in the vitamins and minerals. Cook vegetables until they are tender but still crisp. There are many vegetables which can be served raw, grated or shredded in many interesting combinations. Try a grated apple and carrot salad. Watercress, mushrooms and peanuts, as well as grated cauliflower and mint make tasty and unusual salads.

When you prepare meats, fish or fowl, it is best to use low temperatures which allow the connecting tissue to break down evenly as the heat penetrates. Juices are lost as the actual protein strands begin to get tough and dry. Coat lean meat with vegetable oil before putting it in the oven. Use oven foils as often as you can to seal in the natural juices.

Fresh fruit juices—orange, grapefruit, lemon and berry—are ideal drinks. Sweeten them when necessary with honey. Milk flavoured with fresh fruit juice, or sour milk whipped with lemon juice and a little honey are two nutritious combinations.

The health-food movement has its oddities and, like all movements, indefensible and extreme attitudes. These are now decreasing and show every sign of diminishing yet further. Health-food advocates have many intelligent attitudes towards food and its preparation which are worth following. We are all part of the world we live in. We do not own it. We must live within the limitations of our bodies and of our planet, and learn to accept changes. We should work with nature in a constructive way to conserve and develop what is best, not only for ourselves but for mankind as a whole. We must look before we eat.

Recipes- Healthy & Delicious

A health-food diet is one which is well balanced, varied and composed essentially of fresh and natural foods. The result is frequently a sparkling blend of new tastes, textures and appetizing combinations. These delicious health-food recipes will introduce you to some new ways to prepare food. You will find that the ingredients suggested for the recipes are neither exotic nor expensive, and can be bought in most neighbourhood food shops. The difference is not so much in the ingredients but in the way you cook and serve them.

APPLE MUESLI

Instead of using commercial breakfast foods try making your own. The home-made version is cheaper and more nutritious. Muesli was originally intended as a breakfast food, but it also makes a delicious and nutritious dessert. Instead of apples try other fruits, such as pineapple, bananas or berries.

1 BREAKFAST SERVING
2 teaspoons oatmeal soaked overnight in 2 tablespoons of milk
juice of 1 lemon
juice of 1 orange
1 large tart apple
1 tablespoon honey
2 tablespoons yogurt
1 tablespoon chopped nuts
1 tablespoon chopped raisins

Put the soaked oatmeal in a small serving bowl. Mix in the lemon juice and the orange juice. Grate the whole apple, including the peel and core, into the bowl. Mix it quickly into the juice to prevent the apple from discolouring. Stir in the honey and yogurt. Sprinkle the top with the nuts and raisins and serve.

PISTOU

The secret of a good soup is the fresh, home-made stock from which it is made. This aromatic soup is based on a vegetable stock and is subtly flavoured with garlic and basil. Served with whole-wheat bread and a green salad, it is a complete light meal.

4 SERVINGS
1 lb. green beans, cut in $\frac{3}{4}$-inch slices
1 lb. dried beans, soaked overnight, boiled for 1 hour and drained
2 courgettes [zucchini]
4 medium carrots
2 potatoes
2 tomatoes, blanched and peeled
2 leeks
5 pints [6$\frac{1}{4}$ pints] boiling water
Sea salt and freshly ground black pepper
PISTOU SAUCE
2 garlic cloves, peeled
1 teaspoon dried basil
2 tablespoons olive oil
4 tablespoons grated Parmesan cheese

Wash and slice the courgettes [zucchini] and leeks. Dice the potatoes and carrots.
Put all the vegetables in a saucepan with the boiling water. Season with 1 teaspoon of salt and 4 grindings of black pepper.
Over moderate heat bring the water back to the boil. Cover the pan and boil for 10 minutes, or until the vegetables are tender.
While the vegetables are cooking prepare the pistou sauce. In a mortar pound the garlic cloves to a paste with the basil. Add the olive oil, a little at a time. When it is well blended add 2 tablespoons of the soup mixture. Remove the saucepan from the heat and, stirring constantly add the pistou sauce gradually.
Pour the soup into a tureen. Sprinkle with Parmesan cheese and serve immediately.

HEALTH FOOD SALAD

Don't just make your salads, create them. The art of a healthful salad, which can make a delightful, one-dish main course, lies not in unusual ingredients, but in an imaginative and balanced combination of fresh vegetables, fruits, nuts and cheeses.

Crush the garlic and rub it well into the salad bowl. Combine the oil, vinegar, salt, pepper and yogurt in the salad bowl and mix well. Add the chopped apples and tangerine segments.

Shred and add the lettuce leaves. Chop the lettuce and cabbage cores together, and put in the salad bowl along with the green pepper, celery, spring onions [scallions], radishes and hard-boiled eggs.

Add the broccoli, potatoes, raisins, nuts, cheese, croûtons and toss well. Serve immediately.

6 SERVINGS

1 garlic clove, peeled
4 tablespoons olive oil
1 tablespoon cider vinegar
1 teaspoon sea salt
½ teaspoon freshly ground black pepper
1 tablespoon yogurt
2 unpeeled apples, finely chopped
2 peeled tangerines, segmented
1 Cos [Romaine] lettuce
1 hard, large cabbage core
1 green pepper, seeded and diced
4 celery stalks, coarsely chopped
2 spring onions [scallions], sliced
4 radishes, sliced
2 hard-boiled eggs, sliced
8 oz. [1½ cups] raw broccoli flowerets
6 new potatoes, cooked, cold, sliced and unpeeled
6 oz. [1 cup] raisins
6 oz. [1 cup] mixed nuts
1 lb. hard cheeses, diced
8 oz. [1½ cups] wholewheat croûtons

ANISEED CARROTS

This is an unusual combination of flavours and makes a most interesting vegetable dish to serve with roasted or grilled [broiled] meat, chicken or fish.

4 SERVINGS

1½ lb. carrots
1 tablespoon soft brown sugar
4 tablespoons butter
1 teaspoon aniseeds
1 teaspoon sea salt
4 grindings black pepper

Scrub the carrots well and cut off the tops. If you are using small carrots leave them whole. Large carrots should be cut in quarters lengthwise.

Put the sugar, butter, aniseeds, salt and pepper into a saucepan. When the mixture begins to bubble add the carrots. Stir well, cover, lower the heat and simmer for about 15 minutes, or until the carrots are tender when pierced with a table fork. Serve hot.

MARINATED FLANK STEAK

Rather than dousing your meat, fowl or fish in rich sauces or gravies, let the individual tastes of the meats, herbs and natural flavourings predominate. Marinated flank steak is inexpensive, nutritious and a simple dish to make.

4 SERVINGS

4 fl. oz. soya sauce
2 tablespoons honey
1 teaspoon ground ginger
2 tablespoons lemon juice
2 garlic cloves, peeled
2 lb. thin flank steak

In a small bowl mix together the soya sauce, honey, ginger and lemon juice. Finely chop the garlic and add it to the soya sauce mixture.

Remove any excess fat from the steak. Using a sharp knife make several deep diagonal cuts in the meat.

Put the steak into a large bowl and pour the marinade over it. Let the meat marinate for 4 to 6 hours turning and basting it occasionally.

Remove the steak from the marinade and pat it dry with kitchen paper towels.

Place the meat under a preheated grill [broiler]. Grill [broil] for about 5 minutes on each side or until it is cooked according to your preference.

WHOLEWHEAT BREAD

Home-made wholewheat bread is far superior to any commercial brown bread. Although it is most delicious when freshly baked and spread with butter, honey or cheese, stored correctly the bread keeps extremely well and can be served up to a week after baking. For variation the loaves may be baked in well-greased, earthenware flower pots, or shaped into round or cottage loaves on a baking sheet.

FOUR 1 POUND LOAVES

1½ teaspoons butter
2 oz. fresh yeast
1 teaspoon brown sugar
1½ pints [3¾ cups] water plus 4 teaspoons lukewarm water
3 lb. stone-ground wholewheat flour, sifted
1¼ tablespoons sea salt
2 tablespoons honey
1 tablespoon vegetable oil

Grease 4 loaf tins with the butter.

Crumble the yeast into a small bowl and mash in the brown sugar with a fork. Add 4 teaspoons of water and cream the water, sugar and yeast together to form a smooth paste. Set the bowl aside in a warm, draught-free place for 15 or 20 minutes, or until the yeast has risen and is puffed up and frothy.

Put the flour and salt into a warmed mixing bowl. Make a well in the centre of the flour mixture. Add the honey, the remaining lukewarm water, oil and the yeast mixture. Using your fingers, or a spatula, gradually draw the flour into the liquid. Continue mixing until all the flour is incorporated and the dough comes away from the sides of the bowl.

Turn the dough out on to a floured board, or marble slab, and knead for about 10 minutes, reflouring the surface if the dough becomes sticky. The dough should then be elastic and smooth.

Rinse, thoroughly dry and lightly grease the large mixing bowl. Shape the dough into a ball and return it to the bowl. Dust the top of the dough with a little flour and cover the bowl with a clean, damp cloth. Set the bowl in a warm, draught-free place and leave it for 1 to 1½ hours, or until the dough has risen and has almost doubled in bulk.

Turn the risen dough out of the bowl on to a floured surface and knead vigorously for about 10 minutes. Using a sharp knife, cut the dough into 4 pieces. Roll and shape each piece into a loaf. Place the loaves in the tins. If you prefer a country-style loaf use a heated sharp knife or scissors to make a deep gash on the top of each loaf. Then dust the loaves with a little wholewheat flour. Cover the tins with a damp cloth and return to a warm place for 30 to 45 minutes, or until the dough has risen to the top of the tins.

Preheat the oven to very hot 475°F (Gas Mark 9, 240°C).

Place the tins in the centre of the oven and bake for 15 minutes. Then lower the oven temperature to hot, 400°F (Gas Mark 6, 220°C). Put the bread on a lower shelf in the oven and bake for another 25 to 30 minutes.

After removing the bread from the oven, turn the loaves out of the tins and rap the underside with your knuckles. If the bread sounds hollow, like a drum, it is cooked. If the bread does not sound hollow, lower the temperature to fairly hot, 375°F (Gas Mark 5, 190°C), return the loaves, upside down, to the oven and bake for a further 10 minutes. Cool the loaves on a wire rack.

APPLE PUDDING

Fresh and dried fruits are the best and most natural desserts. This apple pudding is unusual and has a minimum of empty calories.

6 SERVINGS

3 oz. [½ cup] raisins
3 fl. oz. orange juice
    grated rind of 1 small lemon
2 tablespoons butter, softened
8 oz. [2 cups] breadcrumbs, made from
    wholewheat bread
4 tablespoons soft, brown sugar
4 oz. [¾ cup] almonds, chopped
½ teaspoon ground cinnamon
¼ teaspoon ground nutmeg
¼ teaspoon ground cloves
4 tablespoons butter, melted
1½ lb. firm, dessert apples

Soak the raisins in a mixing bowl with the orange juice and lemon rind for at least 30 minutes.

Preheat the oven to moderate, 350°F (Gas Mark 4, 180°C). Grease a 3-pint oven-proof dish with 1 tablespoon of the softened butter. Set aside.

Add the breadcrumbs, brown sugar, almonds, cinnamon, nutmeg, cloves and the melted butter to the raisins.

Peel, core and thinly slice the apples. Put one-third of the breadcrumb mixture into the dish and place half the apple slices on top. Add another third of the bread-crumbs and then the remaining apples. Dot lightly with the remaining breadcrumbs and softened butter. Bake for 35 minutes. Serve hot or cold.

APRICOT SALAD

This salad, made with fresh apricots and served with a tarragon yogurt dressing, is a good accompaniment to meat and an equally pleasant dessert.

4 SERVINGS

2 lb. ripe apricots
DRESSING
4 tablespoons yogurt
3 tablespoons tarragon vinegar
1 tablespoon brown sugar
½ teaspoon sea salt
4 grindings black pepper
    a few tarragon leaves, chopped

Cut each apricot in half and remove the stone. Arrange the apricot halves in a glass serving bowl. Crack the stones with a nutcracker or hammer. Take out the kernels, chop them and set aside.

To make the dressing, put the yogurt into a small bowl and stir in the vinegar, sugar, salt and pepper. When it is thoroughly mixed taste the dressing and adjust the seasoning if necessary.

Just before serving, pour the dressing over the apricots. Sprinkle with the tarragon leaves and chopped kernels.

Why Be A Vegetarian?

People are vegetarians for a variety of reasons. For some it is a question of ethics, a matter of conscience not to kill for food or to let others do the slaughtering.

Other people turn to vegetarianism because they believe that man was not biologically intended to be a carnivore, or because they are concerned with ecology and the balance of nature which they feel is being disturbed in the production of animals for meat consumption. And it is true that about three times as much land is required to feed a carnivore as to support a vegetarian. Some people are convinced that a diet which excludes meat, fish and poultry is healthier, more natural and nutritionally better balanced. Vegetarianism is also one of the tenets of many religions, including Buddhism, Hinduism, Jainism and Seventh-Day Adventism.

Vegetarianism is becoming more widespread throughout the Western world. Only 50 years ago, vegetarians were considered cranks and were the butt of music-hall and vaudeville jokes. About

25 years later they were, at least, tolerated. Today vegetarians are mildly respected. Many current books dealing with nutrition concede that a vegetarian diet, which includes some dairy products, is fully adequate. In fact when a vegetarian diet is properly balanced, particularly when a fair amount is eaten in its fresh, unprocessed state, it has many positive, healthful qualities.

The International Vegetarian Union describes a vegetarian as somebody who "Abstains from flesh, fish and fowl." If they include eggs and dairy products in their diet, as do most vegetarians, they are sometimes referred to, more technically, as ovo-lacto-vegetarians. A small group, who call themselves vegans, do not even eat eggs, honey or dairy products because they believe that the production of these foods involves cruelty. Of course, as with religious adherance, the determination of how closely one follows the stricture of the gospel is highly individual. Many Hindu vegetarians, for example, include milk, yogurt and butter in their diet, but will not eat eggs.

Vegetarians believe that their diet is not only in many ways preferable, but that it also leads to better health. While they acknowledge that for generations man lived without ill-effect on a diet that included meat, vegetarians argue, with some validity, that the affluent society presents new problems. Until fairly recently the majority of the population was not able to afford meat more than once a week. Meat was the treat on Sundays, with perhaps some leftover scraps on other days. Their diet was comprised essentially of wholesome home-baked bread and vegetables from their own gardens. But it was among the wealthy, who were able not only to eat meat more frequently, but also to overeat rich foods, that a high proportion of diagnosed digestive complaints occurred.

As the West has become more prosperous, meat consumption has greatly increased and circulatory diseases have increased, too. Statistics cannot tell the whole story, but they do pose questions of cause and effect. About 40 per cent of the Western world's population die from heart disease. Researchers have discovered a causal relationship between cholesterol, which is found in fatty meats, and to a greater extent in eggs and butter, and heart attacks. Further research indicates that polyunsaturated fats, which are found mainly in vegetable oils, are far less harmful than high-cholesterol, saturated "animal fats."

Many experts believe that by reducing the cholesterol level the chances of developing heart diseases are significantly reduced. Some doctors are convinced that dietary change can not only prevent heart disease, but can also improve existing heart conditions. They encourage patients to eat more fruit and vegetables and less meat and animal fats. Vegetarians, because of their reduced animal fat intake, are less prone to heart diseases, and it has been found that heart disorders are almost wholly absent in populations and isolated communities living on meat-free diets.

Many vegetarians do not eat meat because they are concerned with the technology of meat production. They have misgivings about the antibiotics which are given to poultry to guard against infection, and the hormones which are used to fatten livestock and tenderize the meat. And while modern methods of preserving and canning have greatly reduced food poisoning, meat and fish, particularly in the home, unless meticulously handled, are more prone to the proliferation of toxic bacilli.

In Great Britain, 79 per cent of reported cases of food poisoning are due to faulty preparation of meat and fish, compared to only three per cent from vegetables and fruit, and this is mostly due to faulty canning. When fruit, vegetables or milk "go off" it is far more easily detected. Although they may have an unpleasant taste, the side effects and discomfort suffered if they are eaten are far less serious. In some cases, too, the mouldiness or fermentation produced are even used to advantage as with wine, sauerkraut, yogurt and cheese.

Not only doctors but everyone concerned with nutrition today stresses that we should eat more fruit and vegetables. For most people, fruit and vegetables are merely adjuncts to their meals, which are planned around the main meat dish.

Dr. Bircher-Benner, a Swiss physician who was born in 1867, studied the curative effects of a raw fruit and vegetable diet after he himself was seriously ill and ate, almost by instinct, only raw apples cut into small pieces. In 1902 he founded the now famous Bircher Sanatorium in Zurich. Based on his personal and professional experience and research, Dr. Bircher-Benner formulated seven principles of a healthy diet. Although he did this 50 years ago, most of the principles are still valid and are still followed by vegetarians.

One of Bircher-Benner's principles is that cooking impairs the nutritive quality of food, especially vitamins, diminishes the value of mineral salts and "denaturalizes" it. Although tradition and taste have led man to a preference for cooked food which can be swallowed without difficulty, thorough mastication is essential to health.

Bircher-Benner also believed that in order to grow, keep well and to attain the highest degree of health, man must include in his diet a large proportion of raw fruit and vegetables. He insisted, too, that while people think that they must have their food warm or even hot and may, indeed, derive psychological satisfaction from hot meals, it is doubtful that they are gaining nutritionally. Warmth and good circulation are produced equally, if not more efficiently, by the chemical energy of uncooked food. Obviously vegetables rather than meat are more palatable and safer when eaten raw.

But do vegetarians get enough protein and vitamin B_{12}, the essential nutrients which are predominant in meat? World Health Organization (WHO) scientists are still in doubt about the exact daily protein requirement. They do believe, however, that too much protein is eaten in the affluent West, and too little in underdeveloped countries. Many vegetables, pulses and grains, however, contain adequate proteins and, with the addition of small amounts of dairy products, vegetarians do get more than enough.

In addition, it seems that technological advances will soon bypass the animal altogether. Texturized vegetable protein, known as TVP, extracted from plants and single cell organisms is already being produced. Various blends and prepared food made from TVP, which has the nutritional value of meat and also its texture, are available in health-food shops and commercial manufacture has begun.

Vitamin B_{12} is a problem for vegetarians. No significant traces have yet been found in plants, and although human requirements are small, only one to four micrograms daily, and large reserves are stored in the liver, these can be found in sufficient quantities only in meat, dairy products and eggs. Studies of vegans have shown B_{12} deficiencies in some, although it was found that some vegans developed the cacapity to produce B_{12} in their bodies after a period of initial serum B_{12} decline. But today vitamin B_{12} is being synthesized from moulds, and can be easily taken as a food supplement in capsule form. And some health-food products are enriched with synthetic vitamin B_{12}.

For an adult to adopt vegetarianism is understandably difficult and must, therefore, be based on strong ethical or emotional attitudes. Nobody relishes the idea of foregoing his favourite dishes, and shudders at the concept of living on raw cabbage leaves and lettuce. So would any vegetarian if that were the case! But a vegetarian diet can really be attractive, nutritious and delicious.

Vegetarianism must be given a lengthy trial because the craving for meat subsides only gradually. Some vegetarians believe it is best to eliminate meat

Vegetarianism, when intelligently practised, can be a nutritionally sound way of eating in its own right— rather than a second best alternative to a meat diet.

completely during this trial period. Others feel it is best to start gradually, cutting out first red meat, then poultry and finally fish, while increasing vegetable sources of protein. They also suggest including, at least for a short time, well cooked soups and the more filling vegetarian savouries, which are meat substitutes, and introduce salads and raw vegetables gradually. Of course, a vegetarian diet can be utterly wrong, too, with too much starch, pastry and other sugary things. It cannot be overemphasized that anyone who is a vegetarian or wants to become one should study the principles of nutrition.

The nutrient our bodies most need is protein. Unlike other vital nutrients, protein is not stored in the body and must be replenished every day. The most complete protein foods are meat, fish, eggs, poultry and cheese. But there are many vegetables which, if eaten in sufficient quantity, will supply all the protein needed. The best protein equivalent to meat is the soya bean. Other sources are whole grains (wheat, rye, millet, oats, barley and rice), legumes (lentils, peas and beans), nuts and seeds (pine nuts, sunflower seeds, sesame seeds, pumpkin seeds, peanuts, walnuts, cashew, brazil and pistachio nuts). A

vegetarian must learn to balance his intake of these nutrients. The diet of an intelligent, well-informed vegetarian is not lacking in any of the essential vitamins and minerals.

If you want to try a vegetarian diet begin by substituting for meat, dishes made from eggs and cheese, peas, beans, lentils and nuts and try some of the nutfoods available in supermarkets and health food shops. Instead of fish and meat pastes, meat gravy and extracts, fish and meat stocks, use yeast products and vegetarian pâtés, vegetable extracts, vegetarian soup powders and vegetable stock. Lard, non-vegetarian margarines, animal and fish fats and oils can be replaced by butter or vegetable margarine and vegetable fats and oils. Agaragar and vegetarian jellies are gelatine substitutes.

In a well-balanced vegetarian diet white flour, macaroni, polished rice and white breakfast cereals are avoided. But such natural cereals as stoneground wholemeal flour, wholemeal macaroni and spaghetti, brown rice, wheat germ and wholewheat flakes are far more tasty.

Dairy produce provides an excellent source of vegetarian protein. Cheeses of all varieties can be used in the preparation of hot meals and interesting salads. Milk and dried milk powder can be used in desserts, drinks, savouries and breakfast cereals. And eggs can be used with more imagination than they are in most meat-eater's diets. Yogurt, too, is an excellent source of protein. It can be sweetened with honey or brown sugar and served as a dessert or at breakfast. Vegetarians also make many fruit drinks with yogurt and combined with herbs and seasoning they use it as a salad dressing.

Fresh fruit and vegetables are, of course, the basis of the vegetarian diet. The novice vegetarian quickly acquires a taste for unfamiliar vegetables and begins to experiment with unusual combinations. Nuts, raisins and other dried fruits, for example, are common ingredients in many cooked and uncooked dishes.

But even if you are not considering becoming a vegetarian you can benefit from adopting the vegetarian method of preparing vegetables, which is most nutritious since as much flavour and goodness as possible is retained. Vegetables are washed well, but not soaked, and cooked for the shortest possible time, in a minimum amount of water, so that when the vegetables are served they are still firm and crisp. Also try adding a little oil, crushed garlic, herbs and seasalt to steamed vegetables just before serving.

And if, having weighed everything in the balance, you do decide to become a vegetarian, you will be in the excellent company of such people as Pythagoras, Leonardo da Vinci, George Bernard Shaw and Mahatma Ghandi.

A Vegetarian Diet

This diet has been specially designed for the person who is toying with the idea of trying the vegetarian way of eating. While it is impossible for a diet plan such as this one to do more than skim the surface of the vast range of foods—and consequently of dishes—available to the vegetarian, it does illustrate how the gap left by eliminating meat from a diet can be more than amply filled with interesting and appetizing foods.

But even if you are not a vegetarian, and have no desire to become one, this diet is well worth more than a casual glance. You may be amazed at the variety of dishes given here. For, despite what you might think, a vegetarian is neither eccentric nor ascetic. And a vegetarian diet can and does include a great range of textures and flavours and a multitude of unusual and exciting food combinations. You may find it fun to try some of these vegetarian meals or certainly to substitute some of the dishes described here from time to time.

As for any healthy diet, always buy the best and freshest ingredients. If you start with good raw materials you get the maximum quantity of nutrients for your money as well as the maximum amount of flavour. Green vegetables, for example, wilt quickly. Although they can be soaked in cold water and revived, they are never really as delicious as vegetables which are eaten when they are fresh and crisp.

Vegetarian dishes are no more complicated to prepare than meat dishes. Soups, for example, can be as delicate or as hearty as you like and are very easy to make. Never throw away the water in which vegetables have been cooked because it contains some minerals and vitamins which would otherwise be literally poured down the drain. Use it as a base for your soup stock. Add milk to your stock, or a yeast extract, herbs and seasonings and any vegetables you like, either chopped, grated or puréed. An electric blender is a great asset in the preparation of soups.

Salads, too, are an indispensible part of any vegetarian diet, which can sometimes lack sufficient substances for exercising the jaw muscles. Raw celery, cauliflower, carrots, cabbage and spinach, as well as lettuce, tomatoes and cucumber are all versatile additions to your salad bowl. Tossed in a vinegar, or lemon and oil dressing, salads can be served as complements to main dishes or as a first course. With the addition of slices of cooked cold potatoes, sliced hard-boiled eggs, croutons and chopped or grated cheese they also make an excellent main lunch course.

It is important to include at least half a pint of fresh milk each day on a vegetarian diet. Yogurt, if you prefer it, can be substituted for milk. It can be served plain, or mixed with fruit, nuts and honey as a dessert. It is also an excellent base for a salad dressing or a cold sauce.

Economically, a vegetarian diet has much to commend it. As meat becomes increasingly expensive, more and more people are looking to the alternative sources of protein and fat which are supplied in a vegetarian diet by eggs, cheese, nuts and pulses. But this by no means makes a vegetarian diet second best to a meat diet—from the point of view of nutrition, flavour or variety. On the contrary, many people would argue that a vegetarian diet better captures the full natural flavours of vegetables and certainly in many ways it can be just as delicious and varied as any diet which includes meat.

Sunday

BREAKFAST
Fresh grapefruit juice
Pancakes with maple syrup and butter
Coffee or tea

LUNCH
Thick vegetable soup

Stuffed green pepper
   cut tops off 2 peppers and scoop out seeds. Boil until just tender. Fill with a mixture of boiled brown rice, cooked, chopped onion, mushrooms and sweet corn, cheese and herbs. Serve with a spoonful of yogurt on the top and a tomato sauce
Brussels sprouts and green grapes
Buttered carrots sprinkled with aniseeds

Raisin and nut cream
   raisins, grated nuts and honey mixed with whipped cream and topped with a walnut half

Coffee or tea

EVENING MEAL
Stuffed mushrooms
   stuff 4 large mushroom caps with a mixture of chopped mushroom stalks, 1 tablespoon chopped onion, breadcrumbs, seasoning and grated cheese. Bake in a moderate oven for 15 minutes

Cheese soufflé
Coleslaw
   chopped raw red cabbage, white cabbage, onion, grated carrot, diced green pepper mixed with mayonnaise

Fresh fruit salad and cream

Coffee or tea

Monday

BREAKFAST
½ Grapefruit sweetened with honey
Cheese omelette
Coffee or tea

LUNCH
Fried aubergine [eggplant]
cut 2 unpeeled aubergines into ¼-inch slices. Dip the slices into a batter of flour, milk and egg and then coat them with a mixture of breadcrumbs and grated cheese. Fry the aubergine slices on both sides
Potatoes
mashed with butter and milk
French beans
seasoned with chopped onion

Chilled orange segments
sprinkled with desiccated or shredded coconut

Coffee or tea

EVENING MEAL
Stuffed tomato
cut the top thirds off 2 large tomatoes, Scoop out the pulp and mix it with breadcrumbs, ground nuts, grated carrot and herbs. Fill the tomato with this mixture, replace the tops. Bake in a moderate oven for 30 minutes

Hard-boiled eggs in curry sauce
Brown rice
Dhal [lentil sauce]
Yogurt
mixed with sliced cucumber and chopped mint or coriander leaves
Mango chutney

Raspberry snow
strain fresh, frozen or tinned raspberries through a sieve. Put the raspberry purée in an ice tray and freeze for about 20 minutes. Then beat 2 stiffly-beaten egg whites into the partly-frozen raspberries. Freeze until firm. Serve with cream

Coffee or tea

Tuesday

BREAKFAST
Orange juice
Muesli
Buttered toast with jam or marmalade
Coffee or tea

LUNCH
Savoury scrambled eggs
scramble eggs with milk, butter, seasoning and chopped, green pepper, tomato, onion and mushrooms
Buttered green peas

Baked apple
stuffed with chopped nuts and dates, mixed with honey and lemon juice

Coffee or tea

EVENING MEAL
Vegetarian Salad Nicoise
cold cooked French beans, butter beans or lima beans, chopped onions and stuffed green olives tossed with an olive oil and vinegar dressing

Pizza
topped with peeled and chopped tomatoes, slices of Mozzarella or Gruyère cheese, black olives and seasoned with salt, pepper and oregano
Vegetable salad
raw courgettes [zucchini], raw cauliflower, radishes and cucumber. Serve well chilled with a lemon dressing

Chocolate cream
mix grated chocolate with chopped nuts and whipped cream. Decorate with chocolate flakes

Coffee or tea

Wednesday

BREAKFAST
½ Grapefruit
Cereal and milk
Buttered toast with jam or marmalade
Coffee or tea

LUNCH
Mushroom quiche
    sauté sliced mushroom, chopped
    leeks and chopped celery in butter.
    Mix together 10 fluid ounces of milk
    with 3 beaten eggs, 1 tablespoon
    grated cheese, herbs and seasoning.
    Arrange the mushroom mixture on
    the bottom of a baked pastry flan case
    and pour the egg custard over it. Bake
    in a moderate oven for 30 minutes
    until golden brown. Serve hot or cold
Tomato salad
    sliced tomatoes with chopped chives
    and French dressing

Apple sauce
    flavoured with cinnamon or nutmeg

Coffee or tea

EVENING MEAL
Pea soup

Cauliflower cheese
    pour cheese sauce over whole, boiled
    cauliflower. Top with breadcrumbs
    and paprika and brown in the oven
    Garnish with parsley
Baked potato
    mixed with sour cream and chopped
    chives
Spinach
    seasoned with allspice

Almond carrot delight
    mix finely-grated carrots with ground
    almonds, a little brown sugar and
    single [light] cream

Coffee or tea

Thursday

BREAKFAST
Orange juice
French toast
    slices of bread soaked in a mixture of
    beaten eggs, a little milk and season-
    ing and then fried in butter
Yogurt
Coffee or tea

LUNCH
Tortilla
    fry onion slices, diced cooked potato
    and green pepper. Beat 4 eggs, season
    with salt and pepper and pour over
    the vegetables. Cook slowly. Turn
    out and serve at once
Green salad
    crisp lettuce, endive [chicory], water-
    cress and sliced cucumber in vinai-
    grette dressing

Fresh fruit salad and cream
    tangerine segments, sliced bananas,
    apple, apricots, red plums and
    walnuts

Coffee or tea

EVENING MEAL
Cold artichoke hearts
    with a seasoned mayonnaise dressing

Spaghetti with mushroom sauce
    sauce made with tomatoes, onions,
    crushed garlic, olive oil, oregano, salt
    and pepper and sliced mushrooms
Broccoli

Baked banana
    put peeled bananas in individual
    aluminium foil boats. Squeeze some
    lemon juice over them and sprinkle
    with brown sugar and raisins. Seal
    the boats and bake in a moderate oven
    for 10 minutes. Serve with cream

Coffee or tea

Friday

BREAKFAST
½ Grapefruit
1 poached egg
Buttered toast
Coffee or tea

LUNCH
Tomato vegetable soup

Macaroni cheese
 boil macaroni with coarsely chopped onion for about 7 minutes. Drain and stir into cheese sauce. Garnish with slices of tomato and put under the grill [broiler] until golden brown
Mixed salad
 lettuce, cucumber, tomato and beet-root [beet] with a lemon and oil dressing

Pear
 poached in vanilla syrup or white wine

Coffee or tea

EVENING MEAL
Ratatouille
 sliced aubergine [eggplant], courgette [zucchini], onion and green pepper sautéed in a little olive oil. Add chopped, blanched tomatoes, crushed garlic, salt and pepper and simmer over low heat for 30 minutes. Serve hot or cold

Nut roast
 bind breadcrumbs, ground nuts, finely grated carrot, finely chopped mushrooms, onion, herbs and season-ing together with a raw egg. Pack into a long tin. Bake for 40 minutes in a moderate oven
Cabbage quarters braised in orange juice

Stuffed pancakes
 thin dessert pancakes rolled around a mixture of cream cheese and apricot preserves

Coffee or tea

Saturday

BREAKFAST
Orange juice
Muesli
Toast
Coffee or tea

LUNCH
French onion soup
 garnish with grated cheese and toasted slices of French bread

Russian eggs
 toss freshly cooked and still warm diced carrots, potato, swede [ruta-baga], celery and green peas in mayonnaise. Pile on to a serving dish. Cut 3 hard-boiled eggs lengthways and arrange on salad. Garnish with paprika and parsley

Ice Cream

Coffee or tea

EVENING MEAL
Rice salad
 boiled brown rice, diced red and green peppers, chopped peanuts, raisins and apple mixed together in lemon dressing

Vegetable stew
 to a well-seasoned vegetable stock add whole carrots, new potatoes, little onions, crushed garlic, chopped, peel-ed tomatoes, sliced turnip, French beans, green peas and thyme. Cook until vegetables are tender. The gravy may be thickened with arrowroot if desired
Green salad
French bread and butter

Apple pie
 topped with a slice of Cheddar cheese

Coffee or tea

Calorie Chart

CEREALS, PASTAS AND FLOUR-BASED FOODS

		Calories
Arrowroot	½ oz.	50
Barley, pearl		
boiled	1 oz.	35
Biscuits		
plain [crackers],		
2 biscuits	1 oz.	125
sweet [cookies],		
2 biscuits	1 oz.	160
Bread, brown and white		
untoasted and toasted	1 oz.	70
medium slice from		
large loaf		80
when lightly buttered		135
when fried		185
medium slice from		
small loaf		50
when lightly buttered		85
when fried		115
Breakfast cereal		
such as cornflakes,		
shredded wheat	1 oz.	100
with ½ cupful milk		160
with milk and 2 teaspoons		
sugar		200
Cake, varies according to		
type		
medium slice	2 oz.	200 to 300
Cornflour [cornstarch]	1 oz.	100
Custard made with milk		
and sugar	4 fl.oz.	130
Flour	1 oz.	100
Macaroni, *boiled*	4 oz.	130
Muesli	1 oz.	105
with ½ cupful milk		165
Oatmeal porridge		
made with water	5 fl.oz.	65
Pastry, cooked		
flaky	1 oz.	165
shortcrust	1 oz.	155
Rice		
boiled, cupful	4 oz.	140
pudding	4 oz.	170
Sago, semolina and		
tapioca pudding	4 oz.	145
Spaghetti		
cooked	4 oz.	115
canned with tomato sauce	4 oz.	70

EGGS AND DAIRY PRODUCTS

		Calories
Cheese		
Brie	2 oz.	190
Camembert	2 oz.	175
Cheddar	2 oz.	240
Cheshire	2 oz.	220
Cottage	2 oz.	60
Cream	2 oz.	465
Curd [pot]	2 oz.	80
Danish Blue	2 oz.	205
Edam	2 oz.	175
Gorgonzola	2 oz.	225
Gouda	2 oz.	190
Gruyere	2 oz.	265
Parmesan	½ oz.	60
Processed	2 oz.	210
Cheese spread	½ oz.	40
Stilton	2 oz.	270
Wensleydale	2 oz.	230
Cream		
double [heavy],		
2 tablespoons	1 fl.oz.	130
single [light],		
2 tablespoons	1 fl.oz.	60
Eggs		
boiled, one	2 oz.	90
fried, one	2 oz.	135
omelette, one egg with fat	2½ oz.	145
poached, one	2 oz.	90
scrambled, one egg		
with milk and fat	2½ oz.	200
Milk		
fresh whole	10 fl.oz.	190
evaporated, 2 teaspoons	1 fl.oz.	45
low-fat skimmed powder	1 oz.	90
condensed sweetened	1 fl.oz.	100
Yogurt		
fruit	5 fl.oz.	120
plain, low-fat	5 fl.oz.	75

FATS

		Calories
Butter	1 oz.	225
Cod liver oil	1 oz.	265
Cooking fat [shortening]	1 oz.	260
Corn oil	1 oz.	260
Dripping, beef	1 oz.	260
Lard	1 oz.	260
Margarine	1 oz.	225
Olive oil	1 oz.	265
Suet	1 oz.	260

FISH

		Calories
All weights given include skin and bones		
IF COOKED WITHOUT FAT		
Flounder, plaice, sole	4 oz.	50-60
Bass, bream, brill, cod, haddock, lemon sole, pollack, turbot, whiting	4 oz.	65-90
Catfish, cod roe, conger, gurnet, hake, halibut, kipper, mackerel, mullet, skate, sturgeon, trout	4 oz.	90-140
Salmon, fresh	4 oz.	185
Herring	4 oz.	270
Sprats	4 oz.	325
Eels	4 oz.	425
IF GRILLED WITH FAT		
for each 1 oz. fat, add		260
IF FRIED WITH BATTER		
for 2 tablespoons batter, add		110
IF FRIED WITH EGG, BREADCRUMBS AND FAT		
for each 1 oz. fat, add		260
for each 1 oz. breadcrumbs, add		70
for each egg, add		90

OTHER FISH AND FISH PRODUCTS

Fish cakes	3 oz.	210
Fish fingers [sticks]	3 oz.	145
Pilchards, *canned*	3 oz.	190
Salmon		
canned	3 oz.	115
smoked	3 oz.	105
Sardines, *canned*	3 oz.	250
Tuna, *canned*	3 oz.	220

SHELLFISH

All weights given are without shells

		Calories
Cockles	2 oz.	30
Crab or lobster	2 oz.	70
Mussels, *boiled*	2 oz.	50
Oysters, ½ *dozen*	7 oz.	100
Prawns or shrimps	2 oz.	60
Whelks	2 oz.	50
Winkles	2 oz.	55

FRUIT

All weights given are for whole fruits.
All stewed fruits are without sugar.
For each tablespoon sugar, add 110

		Calories
Apples, *eating, 1 medium*	4 oz.	40
baked cooking, large	6 oz.	65
stewed cooking, large	6 oz.	55
Apricots, *raw fresh, 2 to 3*	4 oz.	30
stewed fresh	4 oz.	25
stewed dried	4 oz.	70
canned	4 oz.	120
Avocado, ½ *medium*	5 oz.	125
Banana, 1 *medium*	3 oz.	65
Blackberries, *raw*	4 oz.	30
stewed	4 oz.	25
Blackcurrants, *raw*	4 oz.	30
stewed	4 oz.	25
Cherries, *raw*	4 oz.	45
stewed	4 oz.	40
Currants, *dried*	2 oz.	140
Dates, *approx 10*	4 oz.	245
Figs, *raw fresh green, 3 large*	4 oz.	50
raw dried	4 oz.	245
Fruit salad, *canned*	4 oz.	110
Gooseberries, *stewed*	4 oz.	15
Grapes	4 oz.	70
Grapefruit, ½ *medium*	5 oz.	15
Lemon, 1 *medium*	4 oz.	15
Loganberries, *raw*	4 oz.	20
stewed	4 oz.	16
canned	4 oz.	115
Mandarins, *canned*	4 oz.	70
Melon, 1 *medium slice*	4 oz.	15
Olives	1 oz.	24
Orange, 1 *medium*	5 oz.	40
Peaches, *raw, 1 medium*	4 oz.	35
canned	4 oz.	100
Pears, *raw eating, 1 medium*	4 oz.	35
stewed	4 oz.	30
canned	4 oz.	90

Pineapple		
fresh, 1 medium slice	2 oz.	25
canned, 1 medium slice	2 oz.	45
Plums, *raw eating*	4 oz.	40
stewed cooking	4 oz.	25
Prunes, *dried*	4 oz.	140
stewed	4 oz.	75
Raisins, *dried*	2 oz.	140
Raspberries, *raw and stewed*	4 oz.	30
Rhubarb, *stewed*	4 oz.	4
Strawberries, *raw*	4 oz.	30
canned	4 oz.	80
Sultanas, *dried*	2 oz.	140
Tangerines, *2 medium*	4 oz.	28
Watermelon, *1 medium slice*	4 oz.	40

MEAT AND POULTRY

			Calories
Bacon (slices)			
fried back [lean], 2	1½ oz.		255
grilled back [broiled lean], 2	1½ oz.		170
fried gammon [Canadian], 1	1½ oz.		190
grilled gammon [broiled Canadian], 1	1½ oz.		140
fried streaky, 2	1 oz.		150
grilled streaky, 2	1 oz.		145
Beef			
corned, 3 slices	2 oz.		130
boiled silverside [brisket], 2 slices	4 oz.		345
minced [ground]	4 oz.		275
roast sirloin, lean only 2 slices	4 oz.		255
grilled steak	4 oz.		345
stewed steak, lean portion	4 oz.		230
roast topside [top round], lean only, 2 slices	4 oz.		285
Chicken, *roast, 2 slices*	4 oz.		215
Duck, *roast, 2 slices*	4 oz.		355
Goose, *roast, 2 slices*	4 oz.		370
Ham			
boiled, lean only, 4 thin slices	4 oz.		250
chopped, canned, 4 slices	4 oz.		390
Hare, *roasted or stewed*	4 oz.		220
Heart, *roast lamb's*	3 oz.		205
Kidney			
stewed	3 oz.		135
fried	3 oz.		170
Lamb			
fried chop	4 oz.		585
grilled chop	4 oz.		435
roast leg, 2-3 slices	4 oz.		330
stewed scrag end			
roast shoulder, 2-3 slices	4 oz.		385
Liver			
fried with flour	4 oz.		325
grilled	4 oz.		170
Luncheon meat, *4 slices*	4 oz.		380
Partridge, *roast, 2 slices*	4 oz.		240
Pheasant, *roast, 2 slices*	4 oz.		245
Pigeon, *roast*	4 oz.		265
Pork			
grilled chop	4 oz.		510
roast leg, 2-3 slices	4 oz.		360
roast loin, lean, 2-3 slices	4 oz.		325
Rabbit, *stewed*	4 oz.		205

Sausage		
fried beef, 2 large	4 oz.	310
grilled beef, 2 large	4 oz.	310
fried pork, 2 large	4 oz.	385
grilled pork, 2 large	4 oz.	385
black [blood], 4 slices	2 oz.	160
breakfast [country], 4 slices	2 oz.	165
liver, 4 slices	2 oz.	185
Sweetbreads, *stewed*	4 oz.	205
Tongue	4 oz.	335
Turkey, *roast, 2-3 slices*	4 oz.	225
Veal		
fried cutlet with egg and breadcrumbs	4 oz.	245
stewed	4 oz.	265

NUTS

All raw and shelled

		Calories
Almonds	2 oz.	340
Brazil nuts	2 oz.	365
Chestnuts	2 oz.	100
Coconut		
desiccated [shredded]	2 oz.	355
fresh	2 oz.	210
Hazel nuts	2 oz.	225
Peanuts		
shelled	2 oz.	340
roast salted	2 oz.	365
peanut butter	2 oz.	180
Walnuts	2 oz.	310

SOUPS

All figures given are for packet soups. Figures for canned soups are usually higher.

		Calories
Clear, such as consommé	10 fl. oz.	40-65
Thin, such as chicken noodle	10 fl. oz.	65-100
Thick or creamy, such as thick pea, cream of tomato	10 fl. oz.	90-200

SAUCES, PICKLES AND CONDIMENTS

Condiments like salt, pepper, mustard, vinegar, spices and curry powder provide negligible quantities of calories in the amounts normally eaten.

		Calories
Bread sauce	1 fl. oz.	30
Brown sauce, *bottled*	1 fl. oz.	30
Cheese sauce	1 fl. oz.	50
Gravy mix, *1 teaspoon*		10
Onion sauce	1 fl. oz.	25
Salad cream	1 fl. oz.	110
Tomato ketchup	1 fl. oz.	30
Tomato sauce	1 fl. oz.	20
White sauce	1 fl. oz.	41

SWEET FOOD

		Calories
Sugar, *1 level tablespoon*	1 oz.	110
Boiled sweets [hard candy]	4 oz.	370
Chocolate		
milk, small bar	2 oz.	335
plain [semi-sweet,] small bar	2 oz.	310

Chocolates, fancy	4 oz.	530
Fruit gums [gumdrops]	4 oz.	195
Peppermint creams	4 oz.	445
Toffees, mixed	4 oz.	490
Jelly [jello], made up	4 oz.	70
Honey	½ oz.	40
Jam, fruit, with seeds	½ oz.	35
Lemon curd	½ oz.	45
Marmalade	½ oz.	35
Mincemeat	½ oz.	35
Syrup, golden [light corn syrup]	½ oz.	40
Treacle, black [dark corn syrup]	½ oz.	35
Vanilla ice cream	2 oz.	110

VEGETABLES

		Calories
Artichokes, *boiled*		
Globe	4 oz.	15
Jerusalem	4 oz.	20
Asparagus, *boiled*	4 oz.	20
Aubergine [eggplant]	4 oz.	15
Beans, runner [green]		
boiled	4 oz.	10
Beans, *baked*	4 oz.	105
boiled broad [dried Lima]	4 oz.	50
boiled butter [Lima]	4 oz.	105
boiled haricot [kidney]	4 oz.	100
Beetroot [beet], *boiled*	2 oz.	25
Broccoli, *boiled tops*	4 oz.	15
Brussels sprouts, *boiled*	4 oz.	20
Cabbage, *raw*	1 oz.	5
boiled	4 oz.	10
Carrots	4 oz.	25
Cauliflower, *boiled*	4 oz.	10
Celery, *raw, approx. 2 sticks*	4 oz.	10
boiled	4 oz.	4
Chicory, *raw*	1 oz.	3
Corn, sweet, *boiled*	2 oz.	50
Cucumber, *raw*	4 oz.	10
Endive, *raw*	1 oz.	3
Leeks, *boiled*	4 oz.	30
Lentils, *boiled*	4 oz.	110
Lettuce	½ oz.	1
Marrow [summer squash]		
boiled	4 oz.	10
Mushrooms, *raw or grilled without fat*	2 oz.	4
fried	2 oz.	125
Onion, *raw*	2 oz.	10
raw spring [scallions]	2 oz.	20
boiled	2 oz.	10
fried	2 oz.	200
Parsnips, *boiled*	4 oz.	65
Peas, *boiled, fresh or frozen*	4 oz.	55
canned	4 oz.	95
Peppers, *raw, 1 medium*	4 oz.	30
Potatoes		
baked old, with skin 1 large	4 oz.	95
boiled, 2 medium	4 oz.	90
chips [fried] from 1 large	3 oz.	205
crisps [chips]	1 oz.	160
instant powder	1 oz.	100
roast, 2 medium	4 oz.	140
Radishes	2 oz.	10
Spinach, *boiled*	4 oz.	30
Sweet potatoes, *boiled*	4 oz.	90
Tomatoes, *raw or grilled*	2 oz.	10
fried	2 oz.	40
Turnips, *boiled*	4 oz.	10
Watercress	2 oz.	10